BOB HARRIS' *Guide to*

STAINED
CONCRETE
INTERIOR
FLOORS

This book is dedicated to my father, Robert Harris II, for his strong work ethic and teaching me to go the extra mile. Also, to my mom, Mary Lou Harris, for keeping her strong family values intact, enabling my father and I to reach our goals.

International Standard Book Number: 0-9747737-0-0

Printed in the United States of America

First Printing: January 2004

Credits

Publisher	Jim Peterson, ConcreteNetwork.com, Inc.
Associate Producer	Lee Ann Stape, Decorative Concrete Institute, Inc.
Executive Editor	Anne Balogh, ConcreteNetwork.com, Inc.
Design	Christina Wilkinson, Sabre Design & Publishing
Photography	Larry Brazil Photography
Publicist/Marketing	Khara Betz, ConcreteNetwork.com, Inc.

Special thanks to Lee Ann Stape for being the spark plug she is; *do it now* is Lee Ann's motto. Also, hats off to Anne Balogh—her enthusiasm and writing skill contributed its own momentum to this project.

Bob Harris' Guide to Stained Concrete Interior Floors is the first in a series of guides for construction professionals on popular decorative concrete topics to be published by the Decorative Concrete Institute, Inc. and ConcreteNetwork.com, Inc. This and other guides in the Bob Harris series will form a collection.

ABOUT THE AUTHOR

Bob Harris is known worldwide in the decorative concrete industry.

He is president of The Decorative Concrete Institute, an organization in Douglasville, Georgia, that offers hands-on training and workshops in the latest decorative products and techniques.

He also was affiliated with a large manufacturer of decorative concrete products for 12 years, the last four of which he served as the director of product training. In this role, he conducted hands-on training seminars in architectural concrete in locations around the world in addition to being responsible for technical support and research and development.

Central to Harris' ability to teach is his extensive experience with the products he trains contractors to use. Prior to his director of product training role, he worked as senior superintendent for six years exclusively in Disney theme parks, doing decorative "themed concrete" work with integral color, dry-shake color hardeners, and chemical stains. On the Disney properties, he did everything from casting tree branches to alligator paw prints in concrete.

He personally placed and/or supervised the placement of over three million square feet of decorative concrete, including work for some of the major Disney theme parks in Orlando, Florida.

Exceeding expectations is what lights Harris up. It could be when an owner he produces a floor for says, "This work exceeds my wildest expectations," or when he teaches a contractor to build floors that will elicit the same elated response from the owners that contractor works for.

Harris also shares his expertise with others through his involvement with industry associations. He holds three certifications from the American Concrete Institute and serves on ACI Committee 303, Architectural Concrete; ACI Committee 610C, Field Technician Certification; and ACI Committee 640C, Craftsmen Certification. He also is affiliated with the American Society of Concrete Contractors and is a member of ASCC's Decorative Concrete Council, as well as the author of several articles for various technical publications.

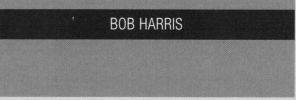

BOB HARRIS

A student is introduced to some of the chemical staining techniques discussed in this guide. The best way to hone your skills is through hands-on training and field experience.

INTRODUCTION

What does a contractor need to know to be successful at applying concrete stains? What are the tips and tricks that I have learned over the years that I can pass on to contractors to save them grief and help them build beautiful floors?

These were the two simple questions I asked myself when I decided to write *Bob Harris' Guide to Stained Concrete Interior Floors* and began to outline the topics of this guide.

While the questions were simple, the answers were very difficult. There is so much involved in building beautiful concrete floors using concrete stains, much that the naked eye does not initially see. Fortunately, I have my teaching to draw from and the thousands of questions students of all skill levels have asked in the classroom over the years. And I have field experience to draw upon, with each job teaching new lessons.

In this guide you will, of course, get solid information on all the basics, including:

- How to prepare samples
- How to establish expectations with the architect and owner
- The tools needed and where to get them
- The multiple ways to score lines in concrete
- Methods for applying stains
- How to seal floors
- The different types of sealers, and how they can influence the look of concrete flooring
- How to maintain concrete floors

But you will also get valuable information on other important topics such as how to protect a floor during construction and prior to the application of stains (your artwork), and why this required protection needs to be in your contract with the owner or it will cost you money; how mix designs, the use of admixtures like fly ash and pozzolans, and textural differences in the finished concrete slab will affect concrete stain application; the various surface conditions that existing concrete can possess and how to handle these conditions; and how to achieve special effects with sandblasting and other tools.

Once you have mastered the techniques for concrete staining, where do you get design ideas? Not every contractor is Michelangelo or Van Gogh. That is why I have included a section in this manual that will point you to all sorts of resources for design inspiration. The ideas are already out there; it is just a matter of finding them. In one instance, I told a student to go to Borders and buy a book on quilts. He came back to class the next day thrilled because on the discount rack he had found three books about quilts with wonderful textile patterns for quilt design – or concrete design!

Be aware, however, that a guide can never replace what you will learn through firsthand experience. I believe there is no better way to learn than on the job site. On the job, you have to deal with other trades, unique job site conditions, delivery schedules, and communicating with architects, engineers, and owners. You have to worry about having power and water, and protecting your work while in progress and after it is complete.

My hope with *Bob Harris' Guide to Stained Concrete Interior Floors* is to provide you with an invaluable shortcut to learning, so you can be a success in building beautiful concrete floors much faster than you might have been otherwise.

BRICKFORM RAFCO PRODUCTS

Some of the most inspired floor designs come when an artist has the ability
to use stains and dyes to express his or her artistic vision.

CHAPTER 1

WHY STAINED CONCRETE FLOORS ARE SO POPULAR

Today it seems that everywhere you turn—whether in a restaurant, retail store, airport, casino, or home—there is a good chance you will see decorative concrete flooring underfoot. In the past, the only place you would find interior concrete floors was in an industrial setting or warehouse, as concrete was considered utilitarian with no aesthetic value.

Interior concrete floors have made the leap from a fringe fashion, a way for artists or loft owners to celebrate their minimalist lifestyles, to an in-vogue flooring material enjoying widespread appeal. The mottled, variegated, natural look produced by chemical staining is often the most desirable feature of concrete flooring.

The widespread appeal of concrete flooring did not happen overnight. Instead, the popularity of interior concrete floors has progressed along with an exponential explosion in concrete coloring options. Each concrete floor is unique, often customized with the input of the owner. When the use of concrete dyes is combined with chemical staining, there are no limitations of a predetermined color palette. Each artisan has his or her own style and inspiration to add to the mix.

The public is quickly becoming very aware of the beauty and versatility of concrete floors. As more concrete flooring choices became available, and as more homeowners and building owners see these choices firsthand and in popular building and design magazines such as *Architectural Record, Dwell,* and *Fine Homebuilding,* the more the public's appetite for custom concrete flooring grows.

Lots of choices with design means concrete is not a one-size-must-fit-all option. When treated with chemical stains, no two floors are alike. The only limitation is the creativity of the installer.

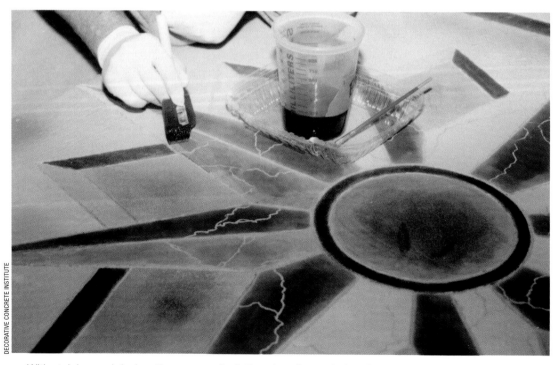

DECORATIVE CONCRETE INSTITUTE

With staining and dyeing, there are no limitations in color or design. The artist uses imagination and a variety of creative application techniques to make every floor unique.

In an entryway, a stained floor makes a grand impression while standing up to heavy foot traffic.

KEMIKO CONCRETE PRODUCTS

Many trendy retail stores are using stained concrete to enhance the shopping experience.

BRICKFORM RAFCO PRODUCTS

11

In kitchens, stained concrete can be a cost-effective, easy-to-clean alternative to marble or ceramic tile.

ENGRAVE-A-CRETE

Here are examples of some of the chemical stain colors available. Each stain manufacturer will offer its own distinct hues.

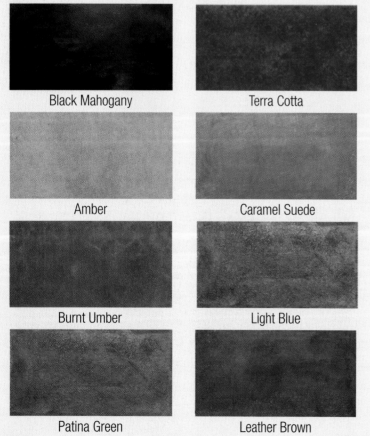

Black Mahogany

Terra Cotta

Amber

Caramel Suede

Burnt Umber

Light Blue

Patina Green

Leather Brown

The popularity of color can vary by region. In the Northeast, the most popular colors tend to be red, green, and golden wheat. In the Southwest, people are seeking striking colors to complement the native backdrops of red and gold.

While the beauty of concrete floors and the ability to customize the floors spark the initial interest in concrete flooring, there are plenty of other benefits to concrete. Concrete floors are cost effective, comparing favorably in price to wood flooring and ceramic or quarry tile. Even the most elaborate concrete flooring designs, with extensive shapes and multiple colors, are less expensive than most terrazzo, marble, or slate—often by a wide margin.

Concrete floors are also clean. According to the American Lung Association, controlling dust mites is very important for people who are allergic to animal dander and mites. Dust mites live deep in carpet and are not removed by vacuuming. Many doctors suggest that patients allergic to mites use washable area rugs rather than wall-to-wall carpet.

With the ability to store and radiate heat, concrete flooring is ideal for those who want to use radiant floor heating. Radiant heat is absolutely the most effective and comfortable way to heat a structure. Concrete flooring is also a central component of passive solar home designs. The concrete slab serves as a radiator, taking in sunshine through properly sized south-facing windows, storing the heat, then releasing the heat as needed when temperatures fall in the evening.

The concrete flooring market is sure to continue to grow due to rapid product innovation, spiraling market demand from homeowners and building owners who want a craft product that is creative and unique, and a growing number of contractors—many with artistic flair—who can expertly install concrete flooring.

Benefits of Chemically Stained Concrete Interior Floors

Beauty	The beauty of concrete floors can be found everywhere, from residences and retail stores to design magazines and popular design-oriented television shows. When seen, the product sells itself.
A Craft Product – Ability to Customize	Each concrete floor is unique, often customized with the input of the owner. There is no predetermined color palette to limit designs. Each artisan has his or her own style and inspiration.
Competitive in Cost	Chemically stained concrete floors compare favorably to wood and ceramic or quarry tile floors. In most cases, elaborate concrete floors are more cost-effective than terrazzo, marble, and slate.
Low Maintenance	Regular maintenance generally involves periodic dust or damp mopping. The amount of floor traffic will determine the frequency of the application of floor polish or wax.
Long Lasting	When installed properly, concrete is one of the most durable materials on earth. Properly maintained, a concrete floor will last for years.
Optimizes Radiant Heat Transfer	Concrete flooring is ideal for use with radiant floor heating because concrete is an excellent radiator of the heat produced by these systems.
Great with Passive Solar Designs	Concrete flooring is often a central component of passive solar home designs. The concrete slab absorbs the heat of the sun during the day and releases the stored heat as needed at night.
Clean	Concrete is a great alternative to wall-to-wall carpeting for people who are allergic to animal dander and dust mites.

Stained concrete is an allergen-free substitute for carpeting in a living room—and the design possibilities are endless.

13

With concrete, "tiles" of any size
are possible to suit
the proportions of a room.

QC CONSTRUCTION PRODUCTS

CHAPTER 2

STAINED CONCRETE FLOORS PROVIDE A WIDE SPECTRUM OF DESIGN OPTIONS

Each chemically stained concrete floor is unique and is often personalized with input from the owner. With chemically stained floors, you can achieve results not attainable with other flooring materials, such as marble, tile, or granite.

With tile, for instance, the installer is restricted to working with fixed sizes, such as 12x12 inch or 24x24 inch tiles. There is no such restriction with concrete. In the concrete flooring world, a "faux tile" can grow or shrink to fit the room (assuming a stone or tile look is desired by the client). The concrete artisan can take the available room dimensions, desired border sizes, and any other design considerations into account and produce a totally unique surface.

Some designs may incorporate straight lines that attract the eye down the length of the line and toward an intriguing architectural feature. Others may stretch the limits of creativity by incorporating arches and radiuses.

When exploring design possibilities, you must consider the characteristics of the existing concrete. In some cases, owners may choose to highlight any existing cracks in the concrete, instead of masking them, to achieve a look that is aged and rustic. Expansion, contraction, or isolation joints can also be incorporated into the design and made a feature of the floor.

Keep in mind that chemical stains and dyes have transparency and are not entirely opaque. After assessing job site conditions, you may decide it is necessary to apply an overlay or skim coat to the concrete surface prior to chemical staining to correct unfavorable substrate conditions. Unlevel floors, heavily soiled floors with rust or oil contaminants, or interior plumbing and electrical line repairs that have been trenched and repoured are examples of where an overlay or skim coat is the best choice to create a new "canvas" to work on.

Sometimes applying an overlay or skim coat is by choice, in order to achieve a certain look. Skim coating or overlaying dramatically expands your color range because the lighter the substrate, the more vibrant or enhanced your staining will appear. Since you cannot achieve white or gray colors with chemical stains and dyes, skim coating or overlaying allows you to start with a clean canvas. It is often desirable to have the lighter underlying skim coat or overlay color show through. In this case, it is not necessary to stain the surface with 100% coverage. Another

KEMIKO CONCRETE PRODUCTS

A diamond motif surrounded by a border becomes the architectural focal point of a room.

15

How Chemical Stains Work

Chemical stains can be applied to new or old, plain or colored concrete surfaces. Although they are often called acid stains, acid is not the ingredient that colors the concrete. Metallic salts in an acidic, water-based solution react with hydrated lime (calcium hydroxide) in hardened concrete to yield insoluble, colored compounds that become a permanent part of the concrete. The acid in chemical stains opens the top surface of the concrete, allowing the metallic salts to reach the free lime deposits. Water from the stain solution then fuels the reaction, usually for about a month after the stain has been applied.

Introducing concrete dyes to your chemical staining project allows you to get into a broader range of colors, such as yellows, reds, and blues, expanding your available color palette. You can even mix colors at the job site to make your own hues. Dyes can also be used to fix problem areas where the chemical stains have not taken. In addition, dyes can soften or brighten up a chemical staining project, if needed.

option is to dilute the stains to enhance the underlying base color. Sometimes faux finishing techniques, such as applying a resist using an acrylic sealer prior to staining, will achieve subtle effects and provide greater depth by allowing the underlying base color to show through.

Diluting chemical stains is another aspect of the installer's tool kit that can provide a much softer look. For example, you can tone down a bright surface, such as a white skim coat, by diluting one part stain with as much as 30 to 40 parts water. Diluting might not always be done with just water; sometimes you may need to boost it with acid to get more of a "bite" on tightly troweled surfaces that are dense and nonporous. It is more difficult for the stain to react with and penetrate these surfaces.

Many different tools and supplies can be used to create graphics and other effects that personalize your floors. The use of different absorbent materials, such as fertilizer, sawdust, and kitty litter, can produce a variety of interesting looks. You can also apply accents of color using

eyedroppers, torn paper, torn edges of rags, feathers, and sea sponges. Additional accents can be created by "blowing" the stain across the surface, using compressed air forced through a fine tip. Decorative sandblasting, acid-gel etching, and engraving are also methods used in conjunction with acid stains and dyes. All of these methods are described in greater detail in Chapter 18, *Specialty Techniques*.

One of the first steps is to determine the best color scheme for your project. Looking at the surroundings, such as the color of the walls, base molding, or window treatments, may shift you to a particular tonal value. For this reason, having a basic working knowledge of color theory is useful in concrete flooring design. Although chemical stains do not necessarily require an understanding of color theory, working with dyes does. Most chemical stains produce various shades of light tan, brown, black, green, or blue green. When diluted, these stains tend to stay within the same color value, simply becoming lighter and less intense. When working with dyes, job site color blending is necessary. Knowing that mixing blue and yellow produces green or that red and blue make purple allows greater flexibility. Using a color wheel is a good way to understand the basics of color theory.

Choosing a design for your masterpiece is next. But where do good concrete floor designs come from? Clearly, contractors with an artistic flair have an advantage. Some of the most inspired floor designs come when an artist has the ability to use stains and dyes to express his or her artistic vision. However, some may find such inspiration difficult to come by. In that case, just look around you, because many good design ideas are waiting to be discovered. Gain inspiration from a book on quilting, a faux painting, decorative wood and vinyl flooring patterns, or the work of well-known architects such as Frank Lloyd Wright and M.C. Escher. Using such sources, along with having

ENGRAVE-A-CRETE

Sawcuts serve as outlines for a bold geometric design in a family room floor.

a basic understanding of color theory, affords the craftsman plenty of ways to add artistic expression to designs. Learn more about where to find design ideas in Chapter 3, *Where Do Good Flooring Designs Come From?*

If at this point you still are not convinced that concrete flooring offers unlimited design options, read on!

Some of the most inspired designs come from artists who skillfully use stains and dyes to express their vision. Introducing dyes to a chemical staining project expands the color palette.

Curved lines and sweeping arches of color direct the eye down pathways through an interior space.

CHAPTER 3

WHERE DO GOOD FLOORING DESIGNS COME FROM?

Rarely are specifications for chemically stained interior concrete floors clear-cut, even on commercial projects. In most cases, clients will welcome your design ideas and even expect them. After all, they are choosing a craft product for a unique look—and you are the craftsperson.

Design ideas are out there in this world. It is just a matter of being alert and collecting good designs when you see them so you have ideas to draw from. I keep a stock of patterns, layouts, and sketches and add to my collection constantly with clippings from magazines, design books, or ideas I get from being out and about.

For example, when traveling I get ideas from the terrazzo or marble flooring I see in airports. If I am in a retail store and see interesting designs in a floor of any kind, I will take notes. Start paying attention and taking notes to document what you see in your daily travels.

Another source of flooring ideas are movies. For example, freeze frame different sequences during Walt Disney's *Beauty and the Beast* and you will marvel at the beautiful flooring ideas.

In a nutshell, good flooring designs will come from everywhere. In one instance, I told a student to go to Borders and buy a book on quilting to glean ideas from. The student came back to class the next day thrilled because he had found three books with quilting patterns on the discount rack. Good ideas can also be found in hardwood flooring books, faux painting manuals, and even books with vinyl flooring patterns.

18

Here are some other resources to get design ideas flowing

Decorative Floors of Venice, by Tudy Sammartini, displays beautiful color photographs of Venetian floors in palaces, churches, and courtyards. These floors are magical and wondrous, as no one floor is like any other. This same magic can be achieved with concrete.

As you enjoy these designs created with brick, Venetian slate, tile, terrazzo, and marble, let your imagination dream up ways to transfer these patterns and techniques to concrete flooring.

Floor Magic, by Alan Berman, explains in detail how to select and maintain flooring that best suits a room and style. Examine the stone, ceramic, mosaic, wood, carpet, and sheet flooring samples for ideas you can translate to concrete. (Cover not available)

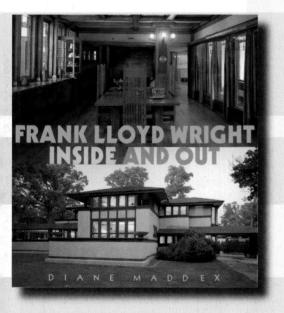

Design Within Reach, a chain of upscale stores offering modern furniture, has catalogs displaying their furniture on concrete flooring or on patterned rugs with designs that can easily be transferred to concrete. Sign up for their mailing list so you can receive their catalogs, or get a catalog online at www.dwr.com.

Each issue of **Florida Design Magazine** (www.floridadesign.com) provides a plethora of flooring ideas for wood, marble, slate, and patterned rugs that you can borrow from to build your database of concrete flooring ideas.

In addition, look through regional design magazines covering your area to gain insight into regional design preferences.

Frank Lloyd Wright Inside and Out, by Diane Maddex, features a collection of famous properties designed by the innovative architect. Many of his designs feature scored, stained, and polished concrete.

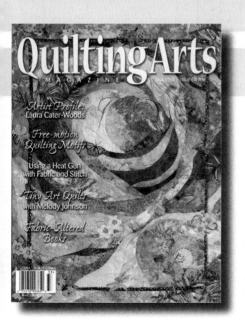

Quilting Arts Magazine (www.quiltingarts.com) not only gives you pattern ideas, but also a variety of good ideas for color combinations.

When I am at the airport, I go into the bookstore and either purchase or look through popular interior design magazines such as **Architectural Digest, Interior Design,** and **Southern Living.** Each issue provides inspiration, color combinations, and ideas that can be used on concrete floors.

CHAPTER 4

BUDGET ANALYSIS OF STAINED CONCRETE FLOORS

While local market conditions, of course, play a large role in pricing, it is helpful to compare concrete flooring with other architectural flooring options. Shouldn't an advanced stain application using faux techniques and complex sawcut patterns be worth as much as wood flooring? I think it is imperative to not only understand where the magnificent concrete floors you are able to produce "fit in" with other flooring materials your customer may be considering, but to also be able to price your work with confidence and without hesitation. As the table on page 22 shows, concrete flooring is an excellent choice in terms of both cost and value.

A basic stained floor (one coat of chemical stain and sealer) is about the same price as inexpensive carpeting or vinyl tile—and will not need replacement.

BRICKFORM RAFCO PRODUCTS

A simple sawcut pattern with
multiple coats of stain
is equivalent to the
price of high-quality carpeting.

THE CONCRETE FLOORING OPTION*	OTHER ARCHITECTURAL FLOORING OPTIONS**
$1.00 - $3.00 per square foot	
Basic one-coat application of stain with sealer (which includes floor cleaning and masking prior to staining).	In this price range, you are competing only against the most inexpensive tile and carpet.
$3.00 - $7.00 per square foot	
Multicoat stain application with decorative sawcuts (such as borders or basic sawcut designs).	At this level, the competition is high-quality carpeting and relatively low-priced tile.
$7.00 - $15.00 per square foot	
Advanced stain application using faux techniques and complex sawcut patterns.	At this price point, you are competing against wood flooring ($8-$10 per square foot) and a range of ceramic and quarry tiles ($10-$12 per square foot).
$15.00+ per square foot	
Adding decorative sandblasting or engraving to the advanced stain application.	The most elaborate concrete flooring options are competitive with lower-priced slate, terrazzo, and marble. A buyer can easily spend $20-$50 per square foot for certain slate, terrazzo, and marble options. Pricing for high-end marble can run as high as $75-$95 per square foot and up.

* All pricing for concrete flooring options assumes that a concrete slab already exists.

**Pricing can vary based on the amount of floor preparation work required, number of edges to install around, color and style selection, and whether the material is in stock or must be special ordered.

Markets surveyed: Seattle, Phoenix, Boston, and Atlanta

More elaborate patterns incorporating several colors of stain and faux finishing techniques are cost-competitive with wood and ceramic or quarry tile.

COLORMAKER FLOORS LTD.

BRICKFORM RAFCO PRODUCTS

Even concrete floors that showcase the most advanced staining techniques, such as decorative sandblast stenciling, are less expensive than most slate, terrazzo, and marble alternatives.

CHAPTER 5

SITE CONDITIONS AFFECTING CHEMICAL STAINING PROJECTS

Site conditions affecting chemical staining projects prior to stain application fall into three categories:

- Project schedules.
- Controlling the other trades who are walking on (and sometimes cutting, drilling, chipping, dripping on, and gouging) the floor that will become your canvas.
- Site issues, such as ventilation, water sources, power sources, and sufficient lighting.

Let's start with project schedules. For each project, spell out in writing the necessary time frames to complete the work—from the initial start-up phase through the application of the floor finish, complete with dry times. If the project has a fast-track schedule, it may soon become apparent that not enough time is available to execute the job properly according to your original schedule. It is much better to know this information upfront, because you can then choose to compress your schedule, if possible, and change your proposal accordingly.

Projects that have flexibility in the schedule still must have an agreed-upon timetable that permits you to complete your work effectively. Sometimes jobs fall behind and schedules get compressed to try to make up for lost time, which can have a devastating impact on a chemical staining project. For this reason, it is imperative to write into the contract the necessary time frames and a schedule for completing the work.

Another critical factor affecting the finished work are other trades who are involved in the project. Understand that most trades see concrete as a slab that gets covered up by carpet, tile, or vinyl. They do not expect concrete to remain exposed as a decorative surface. Precautions must be taken so the concrete is treated during the construction process like it is finished marble.

On a new construction project, determine who is responsible for protecting the floor

Grease or oil spills on a floor will cause unwanted color variations by not allowing the stain to react with and penetrate into the concrete surface.

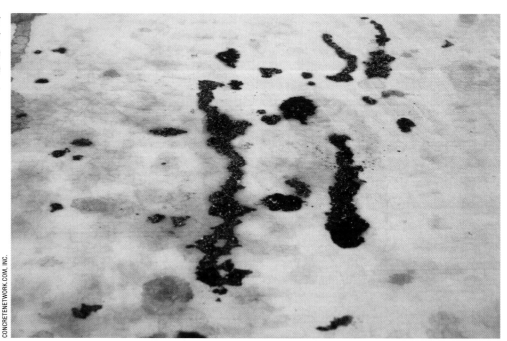

CONCRETENETWORK.COM, INC.

Common Work—Related Issues Caused by Other Trades

Drywall Contractor	If dust from drywall sanding operations gets onto the concrete surface to be stained, it will react with the stain, coloring the surface differently wherever it is present. Drywall mud can fall onto the floor during the drywall taping operation.
Painting Contractor	Paint or caulk that gets onto the floor prior to staining can act as a resist, not allowing the stain to react and penetrate the concrete. If left down too long, certain types of tape applied to the floor will also leave a residue on the slab when removed that will block stain penetration. If paint or caulk gets on the completed work after the staining process, unwanted color variations could occur.
Framing Contractor	Nailing wall braces into the floor can chip or spall the concrete. Framers should brace to the outside of the slab. Framers who scribble notes on the floor with marker to figure out framing dimensions and hardware locations or use red or blue chalk and then lacquer over it may leave permanent marks on the floor surface. (Even if lacquer is not used, water usually won't wash off the chalk.) Framing lumber, roof trusses, and plywood should not be stored on the slab because they can leave residues and change the moisture content of the slab where the lumber rested, which will affect the color of the stain.
Plumbing & Mechanical Contractors	Spills of grease or oil onto the floor before or after staining will cause unwanted color variations. In many cases, the grease or oil will act as a resist and not allow the stain to react with and penetrate into the concrete. Plumber's putty can have a similar effect. If portions of the slab must be removed to relocate or replace plumbing or mechanical lines, the repair concrete may take the stain differently than the rest of the floor.

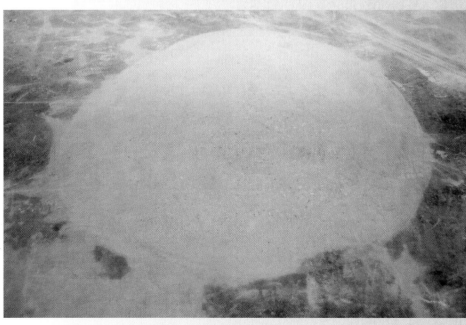

If mechanical abrasion has been used to grind problem areas in a floor surface, the stain will take differently in these spots due to textural variations.

Though helpful in providing information for other trades, the lot and plan number spray painted onto this slab will be a headache for the staining contractor to remove before beginning the job.

Framing lumber stored on a slab can leave residues and even change the slab's moisture content where the lumber rested, which will affect the color of the stain.

during the various construction operations. The bare minimum protection is to cover the surface with a nonstaining craft paper, overlapping the seams. Never tape the paper or anything else to the floor. To guard against heavier construction traffic, consider using Masonite, plywood, or old carpet on top of the craft paper for extra protection.

Another important consideration on the project site is to discuss with the client the need for proper ventilation, a water source, a power source, and sufficient lighting. Proper ventilation is a must for a variety of reasons. Chemical stains can produce chlorine gas, and some sealers have odorous fumes that are not only flammable, but also very harmful to breathe. In addition, the fumes could affect other people in adjoining buildings.

An accessible water source is critical, especially during the cleanup phase of rinsing away the stain residue. Preferably, the water source should be in a location where the hose connected to it does not drag across the finished work; the hose should be kept behind the work area.

It is essential to have a sufficient amount of electrical receptacles close enough to the work area to operate numerous pieces of equipment simultaneously, without tripping the circuit breaker.

For obvious reasons, having the proper lighting while laying out patterns, staining, and sealing is extremely important.

No matter how many precautions you take, however, a slab may still prove to be problematic as a result of unsightly repairs made by others. Often these repairs are not under the control of the concrete flooring contractor and the slab may need to be resurfaced prior to chemical staining, as discussed in Chapter 12, *When Extra Surface Preparation Is Required.*

Be sure to discuss project schedules, other trades on the project, and site issues with the builder or general contractor well before the work begins. Getting these issues out on the table and into the contract is not a guarantee that problems will not arise. But it can help reduce the number of problems that occur.

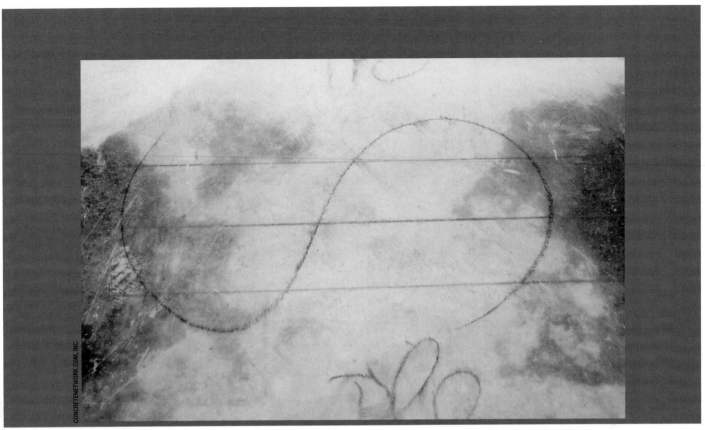

Framers who scribble on the floor with marker to note framing dimensions and hardware locations may leave permanent marks on the floor surface.

Nailing wall braces into the floor can chip or spall the concrete. Ask framers to brace to the outside of the slab when possible.

The optimum finish for chemical staining is a hard-troweled surface. It produces a dense, long-wearing floor that displays color beautifully.

CHAPTER 6

NEW CONCRETE: ATTRIBUTES THAT IMPACT CHEMICAL STAINING PROJECTS

If you are in the fortunate circumstance of getting in on a project early, you can have a positive influence over the concrete you will be staining. The best situation is when you are the contractor pouring the concrete to be stained; then you are in complete control over producing a workable substrate. In most cases, though, another firm will pour the concrete substrate you will be staining. On these jobs, your goal is to have as much influence on the project specifications as possible.

Many contractors do not pay particular attention to the concrete mix design. After the concrete is placed, when it is too late, they find out that the concrete is not reactive and the stain is not taking. Concrete finishing and curing methods can also influence stain penetration and color intensity. The table on page 30 gives some general recommendations for controlling attributes of concrete that can influence the quality of your work.

Often there is no way to predict how the stain is going to take to the concrete. That is why the sampling stage of the project is so critical (see Chapter 8, *Preparing Samples*). There is no use in pretending that as concrete flooring contractors we can get everything "our way." However, the more issues we can influence that contribute positively to the concrete staining process, the better.

More on hard-troweled surfaces

Most stain applicators prefer staining interior hard-troweled surfaces because they can achieve beautiful marble-like effects. I am often asked: How is this possible? Quite frankly, it is simply a function of the way the stain takes to the burnished surface.

Hard-troweled finishes become burnished with each successive troweling. These burnished sections are actually high points on the slab; lower sections do not become burnished. Even though the slab feels like it is smooth as glass, there are highs and lows. The stain aggressively takes where the section has not been burnished but hardly takes at all in the areas darkened from the steel carbon from the trowel. The resulting color variations mimic natural marble.

On the flip side, you may encounter a slab that has been so densely troweled that the stain just sits on the surface with no etching or reaction. It may be necessary to scuff sand or rotary screen to open up the surface. In extreme situations, a combination of sanding and a diluted acid wash may open the surface enough to allow the stain to do its job.

Attributes of New Concrete That Can Influence the Quality of Your Work

Concrete Mix	Generally speaking, the more cement in the mix, the stronger the reaction you will get from chemical stains, producing more intense colors. Therefore, use straight cement mixes, such as a 5 or 6 sack mix or higher, when possible. But be consistent: Staining an area of 5 sack mix concrete that adjoins or butts up to an area made with a 6 sack mix could cause color variations, despite the use of the same stain color. Pozzolans and some cement replacements (such as fly ash and granulated blast-furnace slag) can have positive effects on concrete by improving finishability, reducing permeability, reducing efflorescence, and minimizing color bleeding. But they also can lessen the reaction between the chemical stain and the concrete surface because removing a percentage of the cement reduces the amount of calcium hydroxide (a reaction product of hydrated lime). Metallic salts in chemical stains react with calcium hydroxide in hardened concrete to produce color.
Concrete Admixtures	Most water reducers or air-entraining admixtures will not have a dramatic effect on the final stain appearance. Calcium-chloride-based accelerating admixtures, however, will have a visual impact, typically resulting in dark, splotchy areas. If it is necessary when pouring concrete in cooler weather to accelerate the setting time, consider using a nonchloride accelerator or hot water.
Aggregates Used in the Concrete Mix	While most contractors cannot influence the type of aggregate used in ready-mixed concrete, be aware that some lime-based aggregates, especially if close to the surface, can actually absorb stain and darken the color of the concrete above the underlying aggregates. Also, certain types of aggregates found in the United States are not as absorbent and will not readily accept the stain. It is good practice to routinely test the absorbency of the substrate by wetting the surface with water prior to chemical stain application. In many cases, this simple test can help you determine if absorbent aggregates are too close to the surface. If you begin chemical staining before making this determination, it is generally too late.
Concrete Finishing Methods	The optimum finish, and my personal preference because I like the way the stain looks on it, is a hard-troweled surface. Although open finishes achieved with minimal troweling (such as a broom or float finish) tend to take more stain and produce more intense colors than hard-troweled surfaces, they are less dense, wear faster, and lose color sooner. On slabs that have been power troweled to the point of the surface being "blackened," the surface may need to be opened up by sanding, diamond grinding, or in extreme cases, a diluted acid wash. Use the same finish from pour to pour if possible. Different textural finishes will give you different final stain effects. Also, finish the concrete with hand tools around floor outlets, plumbing risers, electrical sleeves, and other obstructions so these areas are consistent in finish with the rest of the slab.
Concrete Curing	Spray-applied liquid curing compounds should not be used because they produce residual buildup, which impedes stain penetration. Instead, use unwrinkled, nonstaining curing paper. If water curing has been specified, understand that this procedure could trap moisture in the slab. A high moisture content can affect the performance of sealer and topcoats.

BRICKFORM RAFCO PRODUCTS

Metallic salts in chemical stains react with calcium hydroxide in hardened concrete to produce color.

CHAPTER 7

ESTABLISHING EXPECTATIONS WITH THE BUILDER, ARCHITECT, AND OWNER

It is imperative that the builder, architect, and owner know what to expect from a chemical staining project, both the end product that can be achieved and the process of achieving it. In Chapter 1, we talked about the feature of stained concrete flooring that many clients love most: the mottled, variegated, natural look. When talking to clients about the options with chemical staining, have them describe the particular look they have in mind and provide color samples showing the possible variations. As important as the client knowing what to expect is knowing what <u>not</u> to expect: the complete uniformity of a material such as ceramic tile.

Some of your success in crafting an awesome-looking floor rests with the other trades on the project—the people who are walking and working on the floor that will ultimately become your canvas. In Chapter 5, we discussed how these trades and other issues, such as project schedules, can impact your work. Controlling these aspects of the job requires communication and cooperation with everyone involved.

Finally, we talked in Chapter 6 about the importance of getting involved on the project early so you can have a positive influence over the concrete you will be staining in regard to mix design, use of cement replacements and admixtures, finishing methods, and curing. Basically, your clients are buying a piece of art that will be applied to their floor. They do not want to find out about all the things that have to happen to put together a concrete flooring masterpiece while they are under the duress of running their project. You can build a good relationship and avoid problems by providing a solid foundation of information in the early phases of the job.

There is a very fine line to walk in this area of expectations. You absolutely want the client to have all the information necessary to make an informed decision about concrete flooring, yet you do not want to horrify the client with a thousand scenarios of what can go wrong. If you intimidate your clients, they may never again consider a concrete floor.

What you discuss with your client in conversations must be backed up in writing in your contract (see Chapter 9, *Writing a Fair Contract*). Little things may come up that you can readily take care of for your client, such as patching a small area of the slab or spending a little extra time scraping off some drywall mud that spilled onto the floor. But what happens when something unexpected occurs, due to no fault of yours, that ends up costing you thousands of dollars in additional expenses? Accelerated construction schedules are one of the biggest culprits.

In a nutshell: Aim for the top in establishing expectations and building that great relationship with your clients—but cover your back with the contract.

Build a good relationship with clients and avoid problems by providing a solid foundation of information in the early phases of the job. Discuss the options possible with chemical staining, as well as the limitations.

CHAPTER 8

PREPARING SAMPLES

Chemical stains impart a unique look to each concrete floor to which they are applied. This uniqueness is a benefit and a large part of the attraction of concrete floors.

But this distinctive look should not be obtained haphazardly. It is vital to produce a sample of what the floor will look like after it is stained and sealed. Many factors can affect how chemical stains react with the concrete—the quantity of cement in the mix, the age of the concrete, and concrete finishing methods, to name just a few. To achieve the most representative sample for the client to review, apply the sample to the actual floor to be stained.

Here is a checklist to follow when preparing samples:

✔ Review color charts and color chips with the client. Many manufacturers have color charts and sample chips contractors can use as a sales tool and to assist in color selection. Keep in mind that the color charts are on paper, not concrete, and should be used only as a starting point to determine the desired color range. The same holds true for the sample chips that many manufacturers provide. These chips are made in a controlled environment, typically with a grout mix, and will look significantly different than the actual stained floor.

✔ Choose a floor area for the sample that ultimately will not be visible and not part of the finished work. Construct a sample large enough for the client to get a true perspective of what the end result will look like. Small samples do not provide an accurate perspective.

✔ Prepare the floor in the sample area the same way as the actual installation will be prepared (sanding, buffing, scrubbing, mechanical abrasion, etc.).

✔ In the sample area, try to mimic what you are proposing to accomplish on the final floor, complete with sealer and floor finish (wax). By sampling on the actual floor to be stained, you can determine how the stain is taking based on the absorbency and reactiveness of the floor. This will also help to determine such issues as stain dilution rates and the number of stain applications needed to produce the desired effect. Do not stop at the staining phase. Complete the process by sampling the sealer as well.

✔ The porosity of the floor will dictate the amount of sealer the floor requires. If the surface is nonporous and smooth, the use of a lower-solids penetrating sealer may be required or the first coat of sealer may need to be thinned down to make it more penetrating.

✔ If decorative score cuts are to be grouted, the amount of sealer needed to resist the grout residual must be determined. In most cases, two coats of solvent-based acrylic sealer must be applied and allowed to dry overnight before grouting can begin. If there is not enough buildup of sealer and grouting commences, the grout can actually bleed through the sealer and contaminate the concrete surface.

✔ Document the formulas used during sampling, and keep accurate notes in a job file.

✔ Once a final sample has been agreed upon, obtain written approval from the client.

It takes time to properly go through the sampling procedure. But it is extremely important that your clients know what to expect, so they need to see a representative sample.

Sometimes expectations are not met when working with chemical stains due to their variability and unpredictability. It is always best to find this out during the sampling stage.

Many factors can affect how chemical stains react with concrete, so it is essential to produce a sample of what the floor will look like after it is stained and sealed. To achieve the most representative sample for your client to review, apply the sample to the actual floor to be stained.

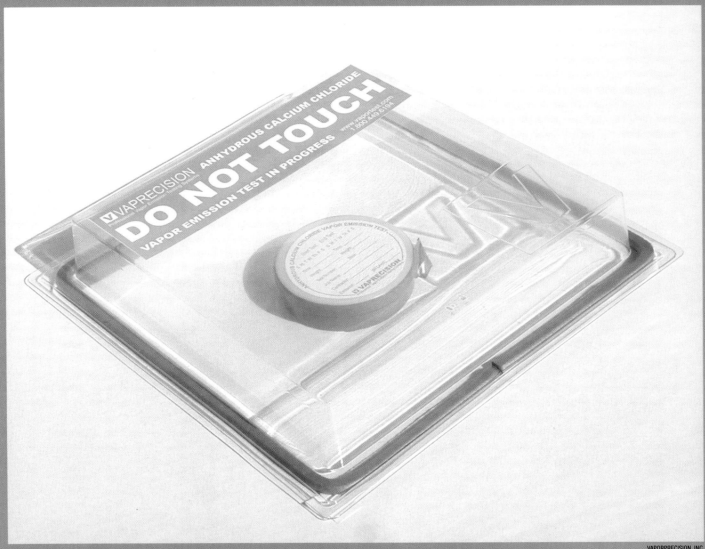

VAPORPRECISION, INC.

During the sampling phase, use a calcium chloride test kit to determine how much moisture vapor the slab is emitting. High levels of moisture vapor emission can affect stain color and sealer performance.

Water absorbency and slab moisture testing

A water check for absorbency should be performed on all existing concrete prior to the application of chemical stain to check the surface density and porosity. A slab may look ready to receive stain, but it could still have a clear sealer or curing agent on it that will block stain penetration.

It is a good idea to wet the floor prior to stain application, if possible. This can be done during the cleaning phase, either with a damp mop or by submerging the floor in water while vacuuming with a wet vac. Pay close attention to any imperfections or resists that could interfere with the chemical staining process.

Moisture in slabs and vapor transmission are big issues in concrete floor construction, and they can certainly affect stain color and sealer performance. You can quantify the volume of moisture vapor emission from a concrete slab surface over time using the calcium chloride vapor-emission test. Having an understanding of vapor emission test results is imperative when working with a manufacturer to select a sealer, since different sealers have different tolerances for moisture vapor emission. Also, certain stain colors that contain copper or cupric chloride have a tendency to blacken or discolor if the moisture content of the slab is too high.

Success with samples!

When going after a project for a huge architectural firm in Miami Beach, I was asked to come in and give a presentation at the client's office. Since I had enough notice, I asked for their corporate logo. They sent a letterhead from which I designed a sandblast logo.

I stained a sample board and sandblasted their corporate logo along with their phone number and address onto the sample. I then put the sample right in front of where the architects in the firm stood in line to get their lunch. As many as 40 to 50 architects touched and felt this concrete sample and didn't even realize it was stained concrete. I ended up getting a ton of work by taking time to prepare this custom sample board. Personalize your sample boards if you have the luxury of doing so.

ENGRAVE-A-CRETE

CHAPTER 9

WRITING A FAIR CONTRACT

I have seen so many start-up and even experienced contractors get burned because nothing was put in writing and important issues relating to the project were discussed verbally or not at all. They failed to get a signed contract, one that is fair and covers all the bases.

Such a contract starts with the well-detailed proposal the concrete staining contractor sends or delivers to the customer prior to being awarded the project. On a residential job, the client usually signs the proposal and the proposal itself becomes the contract. On larger commercial projects, most general contractors use their own contract and send it to the staining contractor to sign. This contract should incorporate all the important issues covered in the staining contractor's proposal.

Here is what a well-detailed proposal addresses:

- Location of the project.
- Who the contract is between (the owner, contractor, owner's agent, etc.).
- A complete description of services to be provided, from any required surface preparation to the floor finish.
- A description of what is <u>not</u> included.
- Provisions for obtaining written approval from the client once a final sample has been agreed upon and before the work starts.
- A discussion of the nature of chemical stains, reinforcing that stains react with the concrete and often are not uniform or predictable.
- Payment schedule.

- The need for sole access to the floor during chemical stain application.
- Drying times for all products installed.
- Start and completion dates of the project, marking the total duration of the chemical staining work.
- Rates for standard work hours and overtime or weekend work.
- How much advance notice is required prior to starting the project.
- Liability responsibilities (general liability insurance, bonding, workers compensation insurance, etc.).
- Any stipulations for cancellation (for example, a designated time frame for cancellation by either party).
- Site issues such as ventilation, water sources, power sources, and sufficient lighting.
- Whose responsibility it is to protect the floor during the various construction operations. It might be a good idea to include a checklist of precautions other trades should take (see Chapter 5).

Fair contracts are a balancing act: The owner must be given all the important details yet not be scared away by a multipage laundry list of possible problems. Having a fair contract does not mean being inflexible; a good contractor tries to work with the schedule changes that may occur. But most contractors cannot afford to compress a schedule into nights and weekends without extra compensation. Put down in writing how to resolve these and other issues that may arise on the project.

Get that signed contract!

SAMPLE
of A General Construction Contract Form

AGREEMENT: as of the _____ Date: _____
RE: PROJECT ADDRESS: _____
BETWEEN _____
(hereinafter called the "owner") whose mailing address is:

_____

(hereinafter called the "contractor") whose mailing address is:

_____

CONTRACT DOCUMENTS

Contract Documents, which constitute the entire agreement between the Owner and the Contractor and are as fully a part of the Contract as if attached, are enumerated as follows:

(Strike through any that are not applicable to this project).

1. This "Agreement and General Conditions".
2. "Procedures for Contractors".
3. Work Write-Up and Itemized Bid Dated _____ ("Specifications and Bid").
4. General Specification Manual.
5. Addenda No. _____
6. Attached sketches/drawings.
7. Owner selection list Dated _____
8. Other _____

THE WORK

The contractor shall perform the entire rehabilitation of the residential structure as described in the contract documents except as indicated as follows to be the responsibility of others:

Scope Responsible Party

_____

TIME OF COMMENCEMENT & SUBSTANTIAL COMPLETION:

The Work shall commence within 7 calendar days of authorization by written Notice to Proceed from the Owner.

The Work shall be substantially completed no later than ___ calendar days from the date of the Notice to Proceed. The Contractor shall be liable for and shall pay the owner $_____ as liquidated damages for each calendar day of delay until the work is substantially completed.

Optional

[If Work is delayed at any time by causes beyond the Contractor's control, then the Contract may be extended for such reasonable time as the Owner's Authorized Representatives may determine.]

OWNER'S REPRESENTATIVE

The Owner's Representative shall be

_____

The Owner's Representative shall:

1. Provide administration of this Contract during construction and throughout the warranty period;
2. Visit the site at intervals appropriate to the stage of construction to determine if the Work is proceeding in accordance with the Contract Documents;
3. Based on evaluation of Contractor's invoices for payment, determine the amounts owing to the Contractor;
4. Have authority to reject Work that does not conform to the Contract Documents;
5. If the Contractor fails to correct defective Work or persistently fails to carry out the Work in accordance with the Contract Documents, by a written order, may order the Contractor to stop the Work, or any portion thereof, until the cause for such order has been eliminated.

CONTRACTOR'S RESPONSIBILITIES

The Contractor shall supervise and direct the Work, using his/her best skill and attention, and he shall be solely responsible for all construction means, methods, techniques, sequences and procedures and for coordinating all portions of the Work under the Contract.

The Contractor warrants to the Owner that all materials and equipment incorporated in the Work will be new unless otherwise specified, and that all Work will be of good quality, free from faults and defects and in conformance with the contract Documents. All Work not conforming to these requirements may be considered defective.

The Contractor shall give all notices and comply with all laws, ordinances, rules, regulations, and lawful orders of any public authority bearing on the performance of the Work, and shall promptly notify the Owner's Representatives if the Drawings and Specifications are at variance therewith.

The Contractor shall be responsible for all safety precautions in connection with this Work. He shall take all legally required and reasonable precautions for the safety of all employees on the Work and other persons who may be affected thereby.

Contractor's liability insurance shall be purchased and maintained by the Contractor to protect him from claims under workers' or workmen's compensation acts and other employee benefit acts, claims for damage because of bodily injury, including death, and from claims for damages, other than to the Work itself, to property which may arise out of or result from the Contractor's operations under this Contract, whether such operations be by himself or by any Subcontractor or anyone directly or indirectly employed by any of them. This insurance shall be written for not less than any limits of liability specified in the Contract Documents, or required by law, whichever is the greater, and shall include contractual liability insurance applicable to the Contractor's obligations under this Section. Certificates of such insurance shall be filed with the Owner prior to the commencement of the Work.

The Contractor shall not employ any Subcontractor to whom the Owner's Representatives or the Owner may have a reasonable objection. The Contractor shall not be required to contract with anyone to whom he has a reasonable objection.

CONTRACTOR "HOLD HARMLESS" WARRANTY

To the fullest extent permitted by law, the Contractor shall indemnify and hold harmless the Owner and the Owner's Representatives and their agents and employees from and against all claims, damages, losses and expense, including but not limited to attorneys' fees arising out of or resulting from the performance of the Work, provided that any such claim, damage, loss or expense (1) is attributable to bodily injury, sickness, disease or death, or to injury to or destruction of tangible property (other than the Work itself) including the loss of use resulting therefrom, and (2) is caused in whole or in part by any negligent act or omission of the Owner, any Subcontractor, anyone directly or indirectly employed by any of them or anyone for whose acts of any of them may be liable, regardless of whether or not it is caused in part by a party indemnified hereunder.

Such obligation shall not be construed to negate, abridge, or otherwise reduce any other right or obligation of indemnity which would otherwise exist as to any party or person described in this Section. In any and all claims against the Owner or the Owner's Representatives or any of their agents or employees by any employee of the Contractor, any Subcontractor, anyone directly or indirectly employed by any of them or anyone for whose acts any of them may be liable, the indemnification obligation under this Section shall not be limited in any way by any limitation on the amount or type of damages, compensation or benefits payable by or for the Contractor or any Subcontractor under workers' or workmen's compensation acts, disability benefit acts or other employee benefit acts.

CORRECTION OF WORK

The Contractor shall promptly correct any Work rejected by the Owner's Representatives as defective or as failing to conform to the Contract Documents, whether observed before or after Substantial Completion and whether or not fabricated, installed or completed, and shall correct any Work found to be defective or nonconforming within a period of one year from the Date of Substantial Completion of the Contract or within such longer period

of time as may be prescribed by law or by the terms of any applicable special warranty required by the Contract Documents. The provisions of this Article apply to work done by Subcontractors as well as to Work done by direct employees of the Contractor.

CHANGES IN THE WORK

The Owner, without invalidating the Contract, may order Changes in the Work consisting of additions, deletions, or modifications, the Contract Sum and the Contract Time being adjusted accordingly. All such changes in the Work shall be authorized by written Change Order signed by the Owner's Representatives and the Contractor.

CONTRACT SUM/PROGRESS PAYMENTS

The Owner shall pay the Contractor for performance of the Work, subject to additions and deductions by approved Change Orders, the Contract Sum of $_____ _____. The Contract sum is determined as follows:

Base Bid _____

Addenda _____

Contract Sum _____

Based upon invoices submitted to the Owner's Representatives, the Owner shall make payments on account of the Contract Sum to the Contractor as follows:

Draw 1 _____ % $ _____

Draw 2 _____ % $ _____

Draw 3 _____ % $ _____

Draw 4 _____ % $ _____

Draw 5 _____ % $ _____

Payments may be withheld on account of

1. Defective work not remedied,

2. Claims filed,

3. Failure of the Contractor to make payments properly to subcontractors or for labor, materials, or equipment,

4. Damage to the Owner or another contractor, or

5. Persistent failure to carry out the Work in accordance with the Contract Documents.

Final payment shall not be due until the Contractor has delivered to the Owner a complete release of all liens arising out of this Contract or receipts in full covering all labor, materials and equipment for which a lien could be filed, or a bond satisfactory to the Owner indemnifying him against any lien. If any lien remains unsatisfied after all payments are made, the Contractor shall refund to the Owner all moneys the Owner may be compelled to pay in discharging such lien, including all costs and reasonable attorneys' fees. Owner may withhold a retainage of 20% of all invoiced charges if the Contractor fails to complete all contract items upon submission of final invoice.

This Agreement entered into as of the day and year first written above by:

OWNER(S)

_____ (signature)

_____ (signature)

CONTRACTOR:

_____ (authorized signature)

Company Name and Address Goes Here

Items in a standard contract (above) are written from the buyer's perspective and provide protection to the buyer. As the contractor, make sure the items listed on page 38 are included in an addendum that is attached and becomes part of the contract.

CHAPTER 10

CHRONICLING YOUR WORK

I suggest that you keep a written record of every project you do. When potential clients see your work and contact you to ask about your wonderful project (which you did two years ago!), you can pull up a database with a record of exactly what you did on that job.

Chronicling your work starts with the first set of samples you submit to the client. If you submit multiple samples that have been fabricated with different stain formulas, label the back of each sample to keep an accurate record. For example: *No. 1 is green stain with a spritz of brown, over a gray substrate.*

The next step is to chronicle the sample you make in an inconspicuous area on the actual floor. This will be more representative of what can be expected on the project, since your first set of samples is just a starting point and will not look identical to the field sample.

Throughout the staining project, be sure to take accurate notes of your work. For example: *First application of brown stain applied one to one, with second application of green stain applied at full strength, wet on wet. After cleaning the floor and allowing the surface to dry, applied two coats of solvent-based sealer followed by six coats of floor finish.*

On large commercial projects, it is extremely important to chronicle the pour schedule and the time frame that elapses after each pour before stain is applied. If you have several months of work involving multiple pours and stain applications, you should try to stain each pour within the same time frame. Staining four days after one pour and seven days after another could produce contrasting colors because the concrete is retaining different amounts of moisture.

BRICKFORM RAFCO PRODUCTS

Throughout the staining project, take accurate notes of your work so you can duplicate the results on other projects (or document what went wrong). I keep design sketches showing dimensions and color selections in a simple three-ring binder.

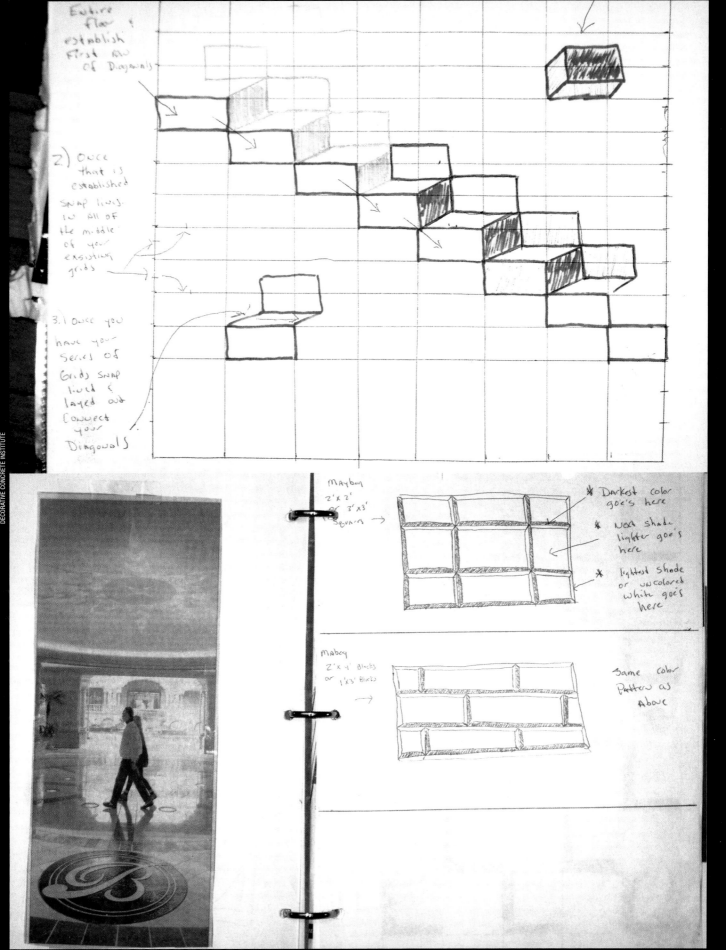

Entire floo & establish First Row Of Diagonals

2) Once that is established snap lines in all of the middle of your exsisting grids

3.) Once you have your series of grids snap lined & layed out Connect your Diagonals

Maybay 2'x2' or 3'x3' Squares

* Darkest color goe's here

* Next shade lighter goe's here

* lightest Shade or uncolored white goe's here

Mabey 2'x4' Blocks or 1'x3' Blocks

Same color Pattern as Above

CHAPTER 11

THE IMPORTANCE OF SAFETY

It is easy to want to gloss over safety and move on to more exciting things. Do not do it. Not only can a disregard of safety procedures prove injurious to yourself, your employees, and other occupants of the structure you are working in, it can be extremely costly if you receive a fine from the Occupational Safety and Health Administration (OSHA) or the Environmental Protection Agency (EPA).

Chemical stains contain corrosive components, including hydrochloric acid and chlorides, that can cause severe eye irritations and skin burns. If chemical stains are swallowed, inhaled, or absorbed through the skin, it could be fatal. Concrete dyes are usually in a suspension of highly flammable solvents, such as acetone or methyl ethyl ketone (MEK).

Following are some precautions to take to protect the people on your projects as well as the environment.

Keep yourself and your employees safe

• Make sure the project has adequate ventilation. If possible, open windows or doors to create air movement; in some cases, the use of a fan may be necessary. Without proper ventilation during the staining process, the overspray can create a vapor cloud that is harmful to breathe. The same precautions apply during sealing, especially when using solvent-based sealers. Make sure fresh air is circulating during sealer application and drying.

• Be aware of your surroundings while working, and make certain no pilot lights, lit cigarettes, or any other ignition source is present that can ignite flammable solvents.

• Wear adequate personal protection when applying acid stains and dyes, including a hydrogen chloride respirator, splash-resistant goggles, impervious gloves, and protective clothing (long-sleeve shirt, long pants, and a nonabsorbent apron).

• Use dust-collection equipment while working on interior floors to control airborne dust particulates that could be harmful to breathe and possibly cause silicosis. Using dust-collection equipment also minimizes cleanup work on the job.

• When using power equipment, it is imperative to follow recommended safety procedures for equipment operation and to wear proper safety gear, such as dust respirators, safety glasses, and ear protection. Check your extension cords to make sure they are properly grounded and have no cut or frayed portions, and be especially careful around water.

• Some stains produce heavier amounts of residue that can become very slick. Use caution when walking out onto the surface to clean and rinse away the stain residue.

Keep other people in the structure safe

• Where possible, keep people out of the structure while you are working.

• Follow the same ventilation precautions listed above.

• Use caution tape or some type of barricade around the work area to reduce the risk of slip-and-fall accidents—and to protect your work from footprints.

Protect the environment

• Capture and dispose of all residue produced by your work.

• Follow all local, state, and federal regulations for proper residue disposal.

Safety is not a game. Take every precaution possible to avoid injury to yourself and others.

L.M. SCOFIELD COMPANY

Workers applying chemical stain should wear adequate personal protection, including a respirator, splash-resistant goggles, and impervious gloves. Chemical stains contain hydrochloric acid and chlorides, which can cause severe eye irritations and skin burns.

CHAPTER 12

WHEN EXTRA SURFACE PREPARATION IS REQUIRED

Upon your arrival at the job site, one of your first concerns should be the condition of the concrete slab. Is it clean and free of defects? If so, then proceed to Chapter 13, *Getting Ready for Stain Application.*

proceed to Chapter 13, *Getting Ready for Stain Application.*

> ### Tip
>
> #### Surface preparation can affect stain appearance
>
> Chemical stains combine and react with the calcium hydroxide in the cement paste at the surface of the slab. If the surface paste has been chemically or mechanically removed during the cleaning process, the underlying fine aggregates can become exposed, which will make the stains take on an entirely different appearance. Typically when staining over such a surface, the final appearance will be more uniform, lacking some of the variegation and mottling you would see if the surface paste had not been affected during surface preparation.
>
> Also be wary of using mechanical abrasion to prepare a surface if adjacent surfaces have been previously stained but were not prepared by mechanical abrasion. Textural differences in the surface play a huge role in the final appearance of a chemically stained floor.

Chances are, however, that some light to moderate cleaning will be required to remove any contaminants on the floor that would impede the stain from doing its job (which is to react and penetrate the surface of the concrete slab). You may find drywall mud, carpet glue, or tile mastic stuck to the floor. Even footprints, dust, or undesirable chalk lines can affect how the stain takes to the surface and should be cleaned prior to stain application. In this chapter, I will explain various methods for removing these contaminants from floor surfaces.

But even clean surfaces without contaminants may require extra surface preparation before they are ready to accept the stain. So this chapter also covers how to patch blemishes in a slab, how to "open up" a slab that is too dense for proper stain penetration, and when to install an overlay or skim coat to correct unfavorable substrate conditions.

Removing contaminants from concrete floors

If contaminants are on the floor, such as grease and oil, paint drips, drywall mud, or caulk, you must first establish the best method for removal. Several factors will influence the method you choose: the type of contaminant, the working environment, and the size of the job.

Simple drywall mud and paint can be scraped off the surface and then removed by a rotary scrubber. For tile mastic, carpet glue, or oil spots, a more aggressive approach may be needed, such as applying odorless mineral spirits and then absorbing the stain with kitty litter. The goal when removing stains or glue is to remove the contaminants without leaving noticeable spots. Be careful when using solvents; since concrete is porous, they can actually draw the stain or glue deeper into the surface. For this reason, a poultice is often a good alternative.

Safety is another consideration. For stubborn stains, you may find it necessary to use a more aggressive type of chemical stripper. Some of these strippers, however, can be extremely hazardous to breathe and apply. If you are working in an environment that is open to the general public, under no circumstances should aggressive strippers be used.

The square footage of the job will also help to determine the appropriate method and type of surface preparation equipment to use. For example, it would be impractical to prepare a 10,000-square-foot slab with a small handheld grinder. The use of a shotblast machine or large grinding machine would better suit a project of this size. Conversely, a large machine would not be practical in a small area, such as a hallway. For tight spots, handheld equipment is the best choice.

Patching a slab

If a slab has flaws that must be patched, it is important to use a patching compound similar in makeup to the substrate. For example, if a self-leveling overlay was used on the slab, use the same material for the patch. The same is true for a skim coat or any other topping.

To patch conventional concrete, acrylic-modified cement-based materials with the right amount of acrylic modifier are a good choice because they will readily accept the stain. Anchoring cement also works well and will accept stain. In most cases, however, these patches will show in the finished product, and the owner should be made aware of this. Even so, a patch that is applied and stained properly will typically cover up an unsightly blemish.

Opening up the slab to accept stain

The main considerations for prepping a surface properly to accept stain are surface density and porosity. Is it a tightly troweled slab that is dense and impermeable? Or does the slab have a float or broom finish that makes it porous and highly absorbent?

If you encounter a dense, tightly troweled slab that will not accept the stain (this determination should be made during the sampling phase), some of the techniques described in this chapter for removing contaminants can also be used to open up the surface. Although some stain manufacturers do not recommend acid washing the slab when preparing the surface for a stain, the use of a mineral acid (such as phosphoric or sulfamic) in a diluted solution can etch problem surfaces without jeopardizing the reaction of the chemical stain. Sanding or screening can also open up the slab enough to allow the stain to penetrate and react.

If you will be staining a polymer-modified overlay, be aware that some of these systems gain strength rapidly. It is important to check the manufacturer's recommendations for the best time to apply stain. Unlike traditional concrete, most of the moisture will cure out of many polymer systems within several days. For this reason, most manufacturers

will recommend staining overlay systems within the first couple of days as opposed to waiting the 14 days required for regular concrete. Some of the techniques described in this chapter, such as sanding or screening, may be needed if the overlay has been down an extended period of time before staining, especially if the system has a high concentration of acrylic modifier.

When to overlay or skim coat the surface

After assessing job site conditions, you may decide that it is necessary to overlay or skim coat the surface to correct unfavorable substrate conditions. Generally, the cements used in patching compounds are much darker and will take the stain differently. Therefore, a slab that is going to require a significant amount of patching is a good candidate for resurfacing.

Consider applying an overlay or skim coat if you encounter:

- Tack strips for carpet around the perimeter of a wall
- Undesirable cracks existing in the substrate
- Areas trenched and repoured for plumbing or electrical line repairs
- Out-of-level floors
- Heavily soiled floors with rust or oil contaminants
- Shot pins or nails installed by framers to hold wall braces
- Excessive chipping and spalling of the concrete

Another reason to apply on overlay or skim coat is to achieve special color effects. When staining or dyeing conventional gray concrete, you are limited in the color intensities you can achieve. A light-colored overlay, on the other hand, greatly expands the available color range. The lighter the substrate, the more vibrant and intense the stain will look. See Chapter 2 for other design options possible with overlays.

See Chapter 2 for other design options possible with overlays.

Special techniques for removing caulk and tile mastic

Two of the most difficult materials to remove from a concrete surface are caulking compound and tile mastic. As with most of the other removal methods described in this chapter, try scraping the area first to remove as much of the material as possible. The remainder can usually be removed effectively with denatured alcohol, applied as a poultice. Once the poultice dries, the caulk or mastic usually has become brittle enough to be brushed off with a stiff bristle brush.

If scraping and chemical stripping do not achieve the desired results, you may need to use mechanical removal methods, such as grinding. However, avoid the use of a diamond cup wheel because the mastic could stick to the diamonds as the wheel heats up. Instead, use a Zec disc (a carbide grinding wheel) that will not collect the mastic as it heats up, but rather throw it off the disc so it can be collected by a vacuum attachment.

Surface Preparation Procedures	Considerations
Degreasers	Commercially sold degreasers can be used for lightly to moderately soiled areas where oil or grease stains have not been on the surface for an extended period of time. The sooner the stain can be removed, the better. If the stain has been on the surface for a while, a more aggressive approach may be needed.
Scraping	Any raised spills on the floor, such as drywall or joint compound, concrete splatters, or caulk, can be scraped off using floor scrapers, putty knives, or spatulas. This removal process is usually done before any additional cleaning takes place.
Sanding pads and screens or Nylo-Grit pads	Sanding or screening opens up the surface of the slab and allows the stain to penetrate. To cover large areas quickly, you can use sanding pads and screens that attach to the bottom of a floor machine. But it will be necessary to hand sand restricted areas where a floor machine cannot maneuver, such as 90-degree corners. Like sandpaper, sanding pads and screens come in a variety of grits. You must determine which grit will give you the best results. The lower the grit number of the pad or screen, the coarser the grit. For example, a 36 grit is very coarse and will remove heavily soiled areas, but it could also leave scratch marks on the surface. A 60, 80, or 100 grit will remove problem areas and is less likely to leave scratch marks. Nylo-Grit pads (which use a nylon designed for aggressive scrubbing and stripping of floor finishes) also work well. These pads come in different colors, each color representing the degree of coarseness of the pad.
Chemical Stripping	If there is residual tile or carpet glue that could impede stain penetration and reaction, scraping may be an option. But in many cases, this method will not remove the entire affected area and chemical stripping may be necessary. Chemicals used for stain removal largely consist of organic solvents that require little or no modification. Some chemicals can be purchased in crystal or powder form and then dissolved in water. Various mineral acids, such as ammonium hydroxide or sulfamic acid, can be used as well. Some chemical stripping agents are mild in their action and safe to use while others can be potentially hazardous and corrosive to concrete, metals, or other building materials. In addition, some strippers are highly flammable. Whatever method of chemical stripping you use, be sure to check the safety and aggressiveness of the stripping agent. This information can be found on the Material Safety Data Sheet (MSDS) for the product.
Poultice	Another method that has proven to be successful is the use of a poultice. This involves mixing some inert fine powder—such as fly ash, hydrated lime, or silica flour—with solvent to make a smooth paste, which is then applied over the stained area. The liquid portion of the poultice migrates into the concrete where it dissolves some of the stain. Then the liquid is gradually reabsorbed back into the poultice, where it evaporates, leaving its residue of dissolved staining material behind. Once dry, the poultice can be scraped or brushed away. Commercially sold poultice materials are available to make your job easier.

Diamond grinding	Grinding is an effective method of removing problem areas. However, use this method with care because the aggressive nature of some grinders can leave swirl marks in the slab. If such marks are a concern, make successive passes with the grinder using finer-grit diamond pads to soften these areas. Grinding can also remove a layer of the cement paste from the concrete surface, which in turn will affect how the chemical stain takes to the surface.
Sandblasting or shotblasting	On areas that are heavily contaminated or soiled, the use of a shotblasting machine or traditional sandblasting may be necessary. An example is the removal of a cure-and-seal compound that has penetrated deeply into the pores of the concrete and cannot be removed by sanding or chemical stripping. Shotblasting is considered a good method of removal but, as with diamond grinding, can leave distinguishable rows or patterns in the concrete surface.
Rotary floor scrubber	After using any of the methods above, do a final cleaning with a rotary floor scrubber.

A handheld grinder is a good solution for removing contaminants in tight areas, such as next to a wall. Connecting the grinder to a dust collector makes cleanup easier.

INTERNATIONAL SURFACE PREPARATION

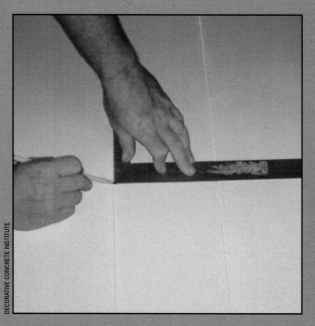

When marking lines for sawcutting, only mark what you intend to cut off so you don't have remaining chalk or pencil lines to clean up later.

Fluorescent chalk is easy to see and won't permanently stain the concrete.

CHAPTER 13

GETTING READY FOR STAIN APPLICATION

The concrete slab is installed, and now it is your turn to get to work. But before you can begin the fun part—actually applying the stain—you must complete the preliminary steps covered in this chapter.

At this point, it is assumed that the other trades have done a sufficient job of cleaning the slab prior to your arrival on the project. However, make sure nothing is stuck to the floor, such as drywall, carpet glue, or tile mastic, that would impede the stain from doing its job, which is to react with and penetrate the surface of the concrete slab. If the slab has not been sufficiently cleaned prior to your arrival, please refer to Chapter 12, *When Extra Surface Preparation Is Required.*

By now, you also should have completed the sampling stage of the project (discussed in Chapter 8), during which a water check for absorbency and moisture testing was performed. Prior to starting work, have the floor installer again check the slab for absorbency to make sure there are no surface contaminants that will impede stain penetration.

Layout and mark lines for sawcutting

The first step is to mark lines for any sawcutting you will be doing. (If your design does not have sawcuts, proceed to the section in this chapter on cleaning the slab.)

The use of watercolor pencils or sidewalk chalk to mark pattern lines on concrete works well because they clean up easily with water. Avoid the use of red or blue chalk since the pigment used in these colors can permanently stain the concrete.

The use of fluorescent or light chalks is recommended.

Try not to overmark your design. Only mark what you intend to cut through with the saw blade.

Sawcut the pattern

Take extreme care during the sawcutting phase of your project, since any overcuts will need to be patched. Usually sawcutting is performed before stain application. But on jobs where color delineation is not crucial, some applicators prefer to chemically stain the entire floor first and then come back and make decorative sawcuts.

In my opinion, the most versatile sawcutting tool on a staining project is a 4 inch angle grinder with a diamond blade. Once you gain confidence using the angle grinder, it becomes the equivalent of your artist's brush; there is not anything you cannot create with this tool.

Having said that, it is not cost effective to sawcut a 4,000-square-foot floor with a 4-inch grinder. But there are plenty of other great options for making decorative cuts. On the next page is a roundup of some commonly used sawcutting tools and recommended applications for each.

>>

A word about laying out designs

Layout and design should be determined by you and the client before anything else happens on the project. When exploring design possibilities, be sure to take the condition of the existing concrete into consideration. In some cases, you may decide to highlight rather than mask any existing cracks. Expansion, contraction, or isolation joints can sometimes be incorporated into the design and made a feature of the floor as well.

Also take into consideration how decorative sawcuts will be terminated. A grid pattern terminating at the wall means getting on your hands and knees with a Dremel tool to continue the sawcuts under the base molding. Putting a border around the perimeter of the wall makes it very simple to terminate dimensional sawcuts.

Sometimes an overhead projector can be used to transfer an image to the floor. Transfer or carbon paper or simple gridding techniques can also be used to transfer images.

Cutting Tool	Applications
Dremel tools	I use Dremel tools with diamond tips for terminating sawcuts up against walls and other hard-to-finish cuts. Dremel tools can also be used for tight-radius cutting.
Core drill	A core drill is an excellent way to cut circles in a slab when the circle's radius is too tight for a diamond blade. I have used a core drill to cut circles ranging from 4 to 10 inches in diameter.
Crac-Vac*	The Crac-Vac is a modified 7-inch grinder that is turned up on its edge and mounted onto a saw cart, so you do not have to bend over and strain your back while cutting. It is ideal for cutting straight artificial grout lines or decorative cuts, and it operates virtually dust-free, using an impeller to force cutting debris into a dust-collection bag.
Mongoose**	The Mongoose is a compact wheel-mounted decorative engraving saw with a powerful high-rpm motor that can quickly make both circular and straight cuts in concrete. This high-performance tool is for contractors serious about stained concrete work or who do not have the confidence to cut freehand.
Wasp Concrete Engraver**	The Wasp is a precision freehand tool for engraving very precise designs into the concrete and for making supplemental sawcuts. The handy pneumatic tool uses a single reciprocating carbide stylus cutter.
Circular saw	Some people prefer to use a basic circular saw for cutting. Keep in mind that this method creates a lot of dust, and the guide on a circular saw can scratch the concrete surface. Rest the saw on top of a piece of Masonite to prevent scratches.

*Available from Sawtec (www.surfacepreparation.com).   **Available from Engrave-A-Crete (www.engraveacrete.com).

The Crac-Vac is an effortless way to make straight decorative cuts in concrete. You don't have to bend over to operate this cart-mounted tool, and it collects cutting debris in a bag as you work.

INTERNATIONAL SURFACE PREPARATION

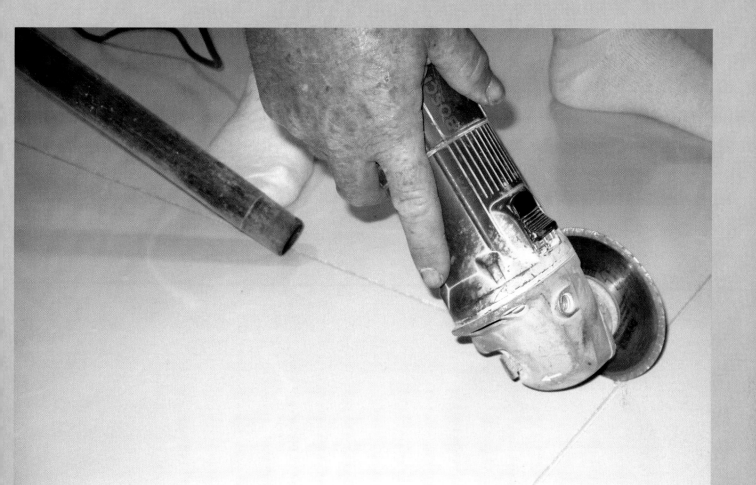

The most versatile sawcutting tool on a staining project is a 4 inch angle grinder with a diamond blade. This handheld dynamo permits freehand cutting and allows you to get up to termination points without overcutting.

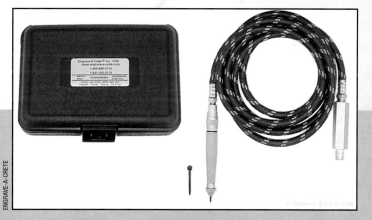

The Wasp is the perfect device for freehand engraving of precise designs and for making supplemental sawcuts. It uses a reciprocating carbide stylus to cut into the concrete.

If you don't have the confidence to cut freehand, supplement the angle grinder (bottom) with the Mongoose (top right). This compact wheel-mounted engraving saw can quickly make accurate straight or circular cuts in concrete. When cutting circles, it's guided by a pivot wheel (top left).

Clean the slab

Once layout, chalking, and sawcutting have been completed, the concrete slab needs to be cleaned. Typically, you can use water and detergent to clean areas lightly soiled by dust, footprints, and chalk residue. In most cases, it is best to use a rotary floor scrubber with a black pad designed for more aggressive cleaning. But first, test a small section of the slab before cleaning the entire surface to make sure the black pad does not mar, scuff, or scratch the surface. If the black pad is too aggressive, use a less-abrasive white or red pad or a push broom and a little elbow grease.

The use of acid washing is not recommended for cleaning the slab. An overly aggressive acid wash prior to chemical stain application can remove too much of the surface paste, which the chemical stains need to react with. However, in some cases it may be necessary to use a very diluted mineral acid wash to open up a tightly troweled surface so it will accept the stain, as discussed in Chapter 12.

The cleaning process lifts the grime out of the slab. Use a squeegee and vacuum to remove all this residual grime off the surface because it can inhibit stain penetration. Also, be sure to barricade the work area to prevent other trades and foot traffic from contaminating your clean surface.

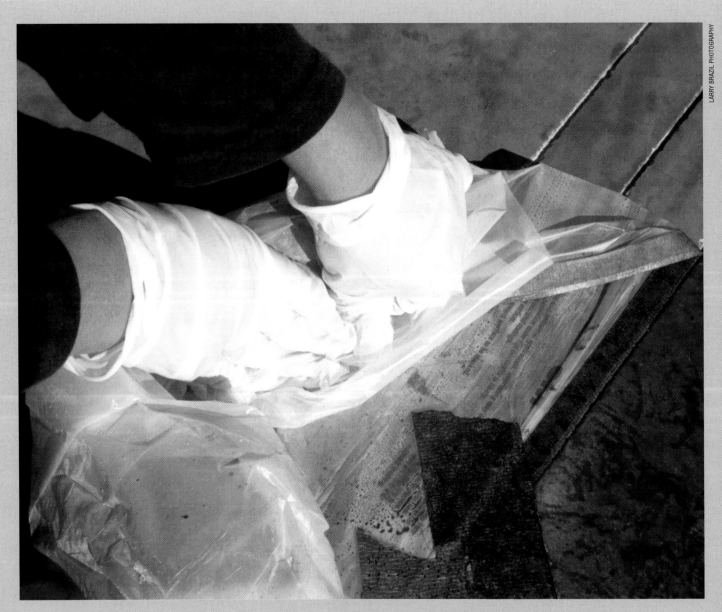

Remove the plastic with care after stain application so any stain that may have dripped onto it won't get on the floor surface. Fold up the plastic, roll it into a ball, and then place it into a bucket for disposal.

Masking

In my opinion, the best way to apply a chemical stain is by spray, after masking off surrounding areas. By spraying rather than using a brush, you eliminate the hard lines and stop and start points produced by the brush strokes.

Never use a high-build tape, like duct tape or yellow fabric tape, to mask off the work on the floor because it could transfer residual mastic onto the floor that will resist the stain. It is imperative to use only green or blue painter's tape, which will not leave residual mastic.

The most important aspect of masking is folding the tape down into the sawcut. This procedure eliminates, or at least greatly reduces, the chance of the stain bleeding. Do not use your fingernails to burnish the tape into the sawcut. Instead, use a painter's hand roller that fits down into the cut.

Use the masking plastic that comes adhered to the tape so the tape and plastic can be folded out simultaneously. Once the tape is down, fold it into the joint and then open up the masking plastic. This tape/masking plastic product can be purchased in different widths.

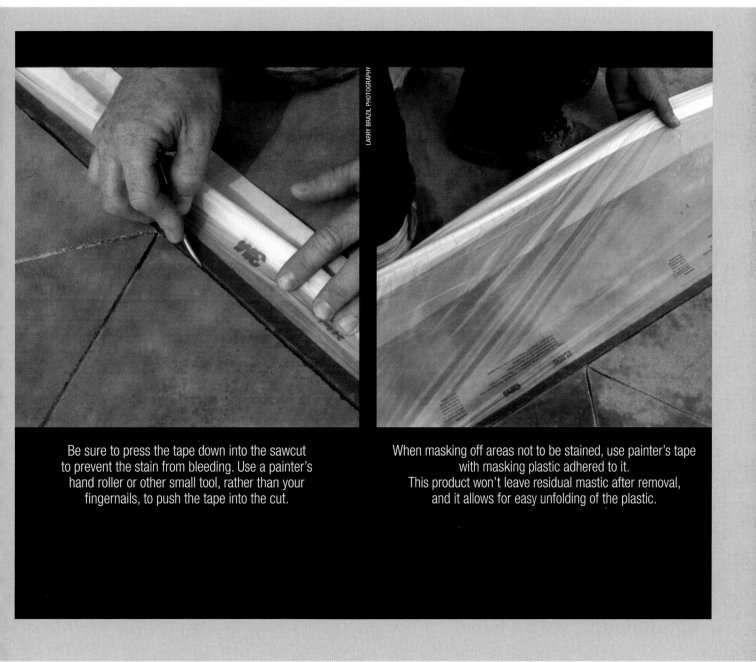

Be sure to press the tape down into the sawcut to prevent the stain from bleeding. Use a painter's hand roller or other small tool, rather than your fingernails, to push the tape into the cut.

When masking off areas not to be stained, use painter's tape with masking plastic adhered to it. This product won't leave residual mastic after removal, and it allows for easy unfolding of the plastic.

It's also important to mask off surrounding surfaces to protect them from stain, including adjacent floor surfaces, walls, columns, and decks.

Special precautions

Once all the masking is down, inspect the masking plastic closely prior to staining for the inevitable little pebble that goes unseen but can tear a hole in the plastic when you walk across it. Later on, during stain application, the stain will work its way through the hole and leave an undesirable spot. As you inspect the masking plastic, put a tape on any holes you find, to act as a Band-Aid.

Also take precautions when removing the masking. Do not haphazardly take the plastic off because if stain dripped onto the top of the plastic (which it inevitably does), the stain can splatter and contaminate adjoining areas. Carefully fold and roll up the plastic into a ball and gently place it into a bucket so you can easily dispose of it without dripping stain onto the floor surface.

Use masking to protect surrounding surfaces such as walls and columns. Make absolutely certain that the stain does not wick or bleed through the masking onto other building materials such as drywall, granite, slate, or tile. For drywall and other wall surfaces, I generally put a strip of painter's tape at the base of the wall where it interfaces with the floor. Over the top of the strip of painter's tape, I apply a layer of masking plastic followed by a layer of duct tape for added insurance. During the cleaning phase, a lot of water is needed to remove the stain residue; the duct tape provides extra waterproofing.

When masking masonry or concrete walls, it may be necessary to use yellow fabric or duct tape first, especially if the wall is cool or damp. This tape has greater tack than painter's tape.

Acids can react with both ferrous metals and aluminum, so make sure that the masking protects metal columns and returns for heating and air conditioning. If possible, remove heating and air conditioning returns before the project.

57

CHAPTER 14

THE CHEMICAL STAINING PROCESS

In most cases, the best way to apply a stain or dye is by using a pressurized spray bottle. With acid stain, it is sometimes necessary to gently scrub or massage the stain into the surface using an acid brush immediately after stain application. Use small, circular strokes or a figure-eight motion when brushing to avoid obvious lines. In most cases, the scrubbing process is not necessary with solvent-based dyes. Some slight scrubbing may be necessary with water-based dyes.

What is the correct age for staining concrete?

Most stain manufacturers recommend waiting a minimum of 14 days after concrete placement before applying chemical stains. The reason is that the concrete can retain excess moisture in the first month as it is curing. Staining before the 14-day time frame has elapsed could produce colors that will not match the color chart provided by the manufacturer.

But what happens if an aggressive construction schedule requires staining within the 14-day window? If you stain immediately after slab construction, the stains will produce much more intense colors because the concrete is more permeable. In most cases, you need to thin or dilute the stain when you are staining new concrete earlier than the manufacturer's recommendations.

Warning: Certain stain colors that contain copper or cupric chloride have a tendency to blacken or discolor if the moisture content of the slab is too high. Manufacturers of these stains often recommend a minimum of 30 to 60 days of curing time prior to staining. If waiting this long to stain is a concern, consider the use of a dye to achieve the desired color. When working with dyes, there are not the same concerns of early application as there are with chemical stains.

Some stain applicators prefer to brush apply the stain straight from a bucket. Be aware, however, that if stain runs down the side of the bucket and onto the concrete surface, it could leave a permanent ring. Setting the bucket in a plastic container will prevent unwanted drips.

Basic tools

Following is a list of basic tools for applying chemical stains. Make sure all sprayers and tools are acid resistant.

- Brushes in various sizes (either foam or bristle) ranging from a 1/8 inch artist brush for detail work to a 6 inch brush for wide borders.
- Sponges in various sizes.
- Acid brushes for scrubbing stain.
- Aerosol and high-volume low-pressure (HVLP) sprayers (for applying dyes).
- Buckets or plastic containers to keep the stain in.
- Various sizes of sprayers, from a hand spray bottle to a 1 or 2 gallon pump sprayer. For large jobs, consider using a backpack pump sprayer that can hold 2 or 3 gallons of stain.

Please refer to Chapter 18, *Specialty Techniques*, for other creative ways to apply stains.

Application procedures

To avoid start and stop lines, always try to maintain a wet edge while applying chemical stains and dyes. One way to achieve this is by dividing the floor into small sections, using expansion and contraction joints as starting and stopping points.

If staining a large area at one time, increase the amount of workers and equipment to make sure that a wet edge is maintained throughout the application. It is important to remember that a chemical reaction occurs between the acid stain and the concrete surface. If work stops in the middle of the floor for any reason, such as a clogged sprayer, and then restarts later, chances are a distinguishable line will result.

Caution

If you clean the slab with water immediately before staining, be careful about moisture remaining in the sawcuts or joints and in low areas of the slab. This moisture can cause discoloration along the joint line and in low-lying areas of the slab, typically making the stain much lighter (or in some cases darker) in these areas than on the rest of the surface. Vacuum the wet areas or take a leaf blower and blow the water out. For quicker drying, use a heat gun or blow dryer.

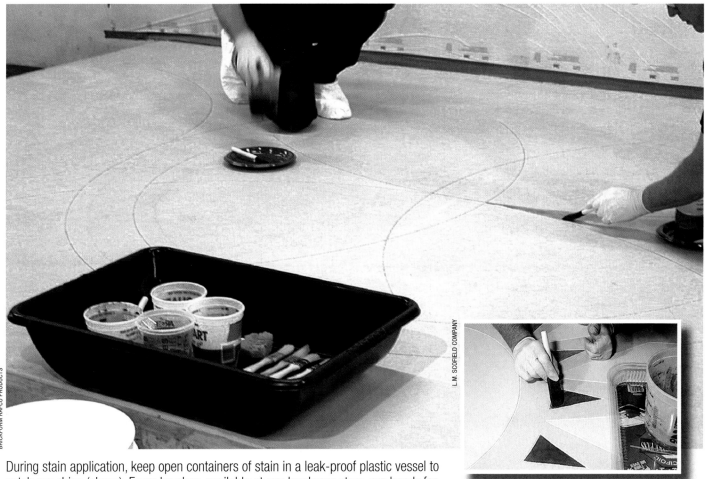

During stain application, keep open containers of stain in a leak-proof plastic vessel to catch any drips (above). Foam brushes, available at any hardware store, are handy for applying stain to small areas. Always wear impervious gloves when working with chemical stains (inset).

On borders, avoid a start and stop line by having two workers start at the same area and proceed in opposite directions, meeting together at the final destination. If you are staining alone, start in the least noticeable place and start and stop at sawcuts to minimize hard lines.

If you are using a sprayer to apply stain, a conical tip—which sprays the liquid in a cone pattern as opposed to a fan spray—produces much better results without leaving distinguishable spray patterns. Don't let the spray splatter unless that is the desired effect.

Splatter can be caused from a lack of sufficient air pumped into the sprayer or from a clogged tip. It is a good idea to run the stain through some type of a strainer, such as cheesecloth, since sediment can collect in the stain container. Always test to make sure that the sprayer is working efficiently before using it to apply stain. Test with water first to make sure a steady stream is coming out of the tip. Have a backup sprayer on the job filled up and ready to go so that you can continue without delay if a problem with the sprayer arises.

If splatter does happen, get the sprayer out of production quickly. Spray a topcoat over the splattered area as soon as possible, not allowing the splattered areas to react and dry before spraying the topcoat. A second coat of stain can also help to hide splattered areas.

It is a good idea to keep a rag and an

Tip

It may be necessary to obtain a saturated surface dry (SSD) slab prior to stain application. This is a fancy term for prewetting the surface (see the glossary at the end of this guide).

Prewetting the surface with water can be effective when staining warm or highly porous surfaces. It cools down the slab and slows the absorption and reaction of the stain, so brush strokes or spray lines don't show as much as they would when stain is applied to a warm or porous surface.

To prewet the surface, mist it with water. Once the water has evaporated, the staining process can begin.

Should stain residue be cleaned if a second coat of stain is to be applied?

The answer depends on the intensity of the stain being used and the absorbency of the slab. If applying full-strength stain (undiluted) in colors such as dark brown or brick terra cotta, which tend to leave a tremendous amount of residue, you will need to clean the slab and let it dry prior to applying the second coat of stain. If you skip this step, a good percentage of the second coat of stain will just lie on top of the first coat's residue and not be able to fully react.

Conversely, if the stain has been diluted or has a higher acid concentration (as light tan and green stains do), there may not be much residue left on the surface, making it unnecessary to clean the slab before applying a second coat of stain.

As a general rule, darker stain colors will produce more residue than lighter colors. Since each slab accepts and reacts with stain differently, evaluate the slab and see how much residue is left on the surface after the first coat of stain to determine whether cleaning is needed before the second coat.

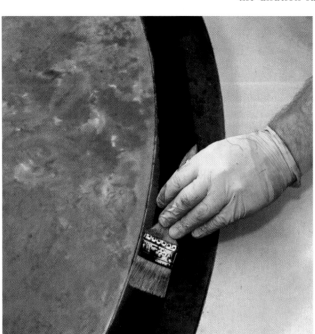

If using a bristle brush to apply stain, make sure the bristles are acid resistant.

empty bucket close at hand. I have seen problems with sprayers sticking in the "on" position and the handle will not release. If this occurs, wrap the tip in a rag, put the sprayer into the bucket, and quickly depressurize the sprayer.

It is extremely important while spraying stain never to get the tip too close to the surface of the concrete. Spray at a distance no closer than 12 inches. Otherwise, dark splotches can occur from the stain reacting too quickly. The stain can actually burn the slab, leaving permanent dark areas. It also is important to keep the sprayer pumped and fully pressurized to atomize the stain as it comes out of the sprayer.

When to dilute stains

Some concrete surfaces, as well as some skim coats and overlays, are highly absorbent and the stain will take to them aggressively. Some of the darker stain colors will produce so much residue when used full strength on absorbent surfaces that you are likely to see brush strokes or spray lines. Diluting the first coat will not only dilute the color, but also the reaction. Dilution will give you a much softer look or allow you to build up color in stages to achieve the desired effect. For other tips on diluting stains to achieve special effects, see Chapter 2.

You can dilute stains with water or acid. Diluting with acid gives the stain more bite on nonporous surfaces. Regardless of the dilution rate or stain formula used, it is imperative to conduct a test sample on the actual concrete to be stained using the proposed method of application to check the stain's suitability with the substrate.

Keep in mind that some stain colors are deceiving in liquid form. For example, a stain may look green in its container but will take on its actual color after it has reacted with the concrete surface, ultimately turning into a medium or dark brown. In the case of dyes, there is more flexibility in the end color because dyes are packaged in concentrated form and there is no chemical reaction, as with a stain.

Applying a second coat of stain

Many projects require only one coat of stain. But you may determine during the sampling phase of the project (see Chapter 8) that a second coat of stain is needed. If so, follow the same procedures given in this chapter for applying the first coat.

There are several reasons for using a second coat of stain. The most obvious is to increase the intensity of the color. After applying one coat of stain and cleaning off the residue, you may decide that a darker or richer color is needed.

Another reason for a second coat of stain is to hide brush strokes or spray lines left from the first coat. These marks can be especially evident on highly absorbent surfaces. A second coat will usually cover them up.

A second coat of stain can also fix areas where the first coat of stain did not take. These problem areas often are very blotchy, almost like leopard skin. Spot staining can help the floor blend more uniformly.

Cleaning up residual stain

It is very important to clean the slab thoroughly after staining so the sealer will bond when applied to the slab. Typically, you should wait to remove stain until the chemical reaction is complete, generally a minimum of three to four hours after the stain application. Sometimes you may need to remove the stain much sooner to achieve a desired effect. Conversely, substrates in a cool, damp environment may require a longer wait because of the increased drying time.

The intent of cleaning is to get the surface free of contaminants while neutralizing the surface. The stain residue must be removed and the stain neutralized using ammonia, baking soda, and water or by using prepackaged neutralizing packs mixed with water. Trisodium phosphate (TSP) also

Once the chemical reaction of the stain is complete, it's important to scrub off the stain residue and neutralize the stain so the sealer will bond properly. If possible, have one person handle the broom or floor scrubber while another person uses a wet vac to pull up the residue.

To avoid start and stop lines while applying chemical stains, work in smaller sections separated by joints or sawcuts when possible. Don't stop work in the middle of the floor for any reason.

works well. For certain sealers the pH level could be an issue, so check with the sealer manufacturer for recommendations.

There are several ways to properly clean the floor. The residue can be scrubbed off aggressively with brooms and muscle power. Or you can use a floor scrubber with a white pad or soft bassine bristles. In any case, make sure your method of cleaning is not too aggressive. If using a floor scrubber, turn the machine on and off and inspect the area to make sure stain is not being removed due

to overaggressiveness. On large projects, the use of a commercial-grade floor scrubber will help expedite the cleaning process. Use a wet vac to vacuum up all residue as you clean.

Once you begin the scrubbing process, it is imperative to keep the floor wet and not let the residue dry. Also, do not track wet residue across a dry floor; it may be difficult to remove footprints on some substrates. It is a good idea to have one person handling the scrubbing machine or broom, one person operating the vacuum, and another person following behind the cleaning process with clean water and a mop.

Check to make sure that the residue is indeed being lifted from the surface. Once you feel you have done a thorough job of cleaning, perform the "white glove" test. Dampen a white terry cloth T-shirt or rag in a bucket of water and ring it out. Then gently rub it across the concrete surface. If the rag stays clean, the surface should accept the sealer without any adherence problems. If the rag becomes contaminated with stain residue, clean the floor again until it is fully clean.

The white glove test does not lie. Although it may be difficult to obtain a totally clean rag when using certain stain colors on certain substrates, the majority of the rag should stay clean.

When applied full strength, dyes can produce dramatic color accents,
such as this border stripe (above).
An artisan applied the dye with a low-pressure sprayer (right)
while other crewmembers held a paint shield
to protect the stained portions of the slab.

CHAPTER 15

APPLYING DYES AND GROUT

Concrete dyes and grout can further enhance your chemical staining projects and open up a whole new set of design options. Here are some tips for using each.

Dyes

Dyes have a multitude of applications. Translucent in color, they can soften areas of the slab where the chemical stain has produced an overly bright tone. They can also be used to enhance stain colors in areas of the slab where the stain is not reacting with the concrete and the color needs to be intensified. When applied full strength and in successive coats, dyes can become nearly solid in color.

When using dyes, you are not limited by a predetermined color palette. They can produce bright, vibrant colors such as

After the grout has dried, use a rotary floor buffer to remove any excess material and then sweep or vacuum the area. On smaller jobs or in restricted areas, you can loosen grout residue by dry rubbing with a piece of burlap or denim.

 yellows and blues, and you can mix your own custom colors on the job site. Unlike stains, dyes are not chemically reactive with concrete; instead, the fine coloring agents in dyes penetrate the concrete surface. Some dyes can be diluted with water or solvents to improve penetration.

Dyes can be applied in a variety of ways, similar to how chemical stains are applied (covered in Chapter 14). Before commencing dye application, wait until the stain achieves the desired look and intensity, cleaning is complete, and the floor is dry.

Grout

Aesthetics is the number one reason to grout joints and sawcuts in chemically stained concrete floors. Grouting the floor defines the lines, gives dimension and depth to sawcuts, and defines the color patterns of the stain and dye. Using grout colors that contrast with the stain and dye can produce remarkable artistic expression. Grouting may also be required for hygienic purposes, in environments such as food preparation areas.

The concrete slab must be sealed prior to grout application. If sealing is not done and grouting commences, the grout residue will permanently contaminate the concrete substrate. Note, however, that the slab will need to be sealed again later after the project is complete. For more information on applying sealers and the considerations for choosing a sealer, see Chapter 16, *Sealing and Protecting Your Work*.

Prior to sealing, there should be no stain residue on the floor and dyes should have already been applied if they are part of the project. The floor should be totally dry.

In most cases, there is no reason to reclean the floor after dye application because dye particles are very fine and absorbed into the surface. However, if water-based dyes are used, it may be necessary to spot clean any residue left from the dyes.

Using grout in a contrasting color accentuates stain designs and adds dimension. For this job, a black tile grout is being applied with a grout float.

(see Chapter 8)

> ## Tip
>
> Prior to sealing, make sure no standing water is in joints or sawcuts and that sawcut edges are not darker due to moisture. In most cases, once the slab is sealed, those areas will retain the moisture and remain darkened permanently. Use a heat gun, blow dryer, or leaf blower to thoroughly dry these areas.

The amount of sealer required depends on how absorbent the floor is and the solids content of the sealer being used. If the floor is porous, it may require two coats of sealer prior to grouting. If using a low-solids water-based or solvent-based sealer on a porous surface, it is almost guaranteed that the surface will require two coats of sealer prior to grouting. But if the slab surface is smooth and the sealer has a solids content of 20% to 25%, one coat of sealer may be sufficient.

Some installers prefer to thin the first coat of sealer, depending on the solids content, so it will penetrate into the pores of the concrete more readily. This coat is sometimes referred to as a "hot coat." It is best to predetermine the amount of sealer needed during the sampling phase of the project, not when the job is in progress (see Chapter 8). Let the sealer dry at least overnight or preferably 24 hours prior to grout installation.

Grout can be purchased preblended in a multitude of colors. Simply add water to the preblended grout to achieve a creamy consistency. Several different methods can be used to apply the grout into the joint or sawcut, but one of the most popular is to use a sponge designed for grouting ceramic tile, such as a red rubber or black foam sponge.

Once the grout has hazed over (dried to a lighter color), remove the remaining grout adhering to the sides of the joint. You can loosen it by dry rubbing with a piece of burlap or denim and then sweeping or vacuuming up the residue. Or, after the grout has dried sufficiently (usually about 30 to 60 minutes after being applied, depending on site conditions), use a rotary floor buffer with a white pad to buff off the dry grout. Follow up by sweeping or vacuuming the area. In most cases, it will be necessary to use a damp sponge to go over the top of the joint to clean any lingering grout residue and to help cure the grout remaining in the joint.

For best results, allow the grout to dry overnight or a minimum of eight hours before final sealer application to avoid trapping in moisture.

> ## Tip
>
> For working joints where the slab may exhibit movement, such as isolation or contraction joints, use an elastomeric caulk instead of grout.

CHAPTER 16

SEALING AND PROTECTING YOUR WORK

If you can seal and protect your stained concrete project before other trades continue work in the area, it can save on cleanup and minimize damage to the floor surface.

After the grout has dried (overnight or for a minimum of eight hours), the final coat of sealer can be applied. However, make sure the sealer has sufficient time to fully dry and cure before you apply the floor finish. Some water-based sealers, if covered too soon, can lock in moisture, causing the sealer to whiten.

Considerations in selecting a sealer

Although many types of sealers are available, three primary types are used for interior slabs: acrylics, urethanes, and epoxies. A general overview of these sealers is provided here. Check with the sealer manufacturer for recommendations as to the appropriate sealer to use for a particular application as well as installation instructions.

Here are some critical factors to consider when selecting a sealer:

- Breathability (the ability of the sealer to allow moisture in the slab to escape)
- Durability
- Abrasion resistance
- UV stability
- Ease of application
- Finish desired (wet look, matte, etc.)
- Cost

Most acrylic sealers (either solvent or water based) are breathable, easy to apply, and inexpensive. Generally, acrylic sealers have a softer surface than urethanes or epoxies, thus they are not as durable.

Urethane sealers provide an abrasion-resistant surface but most are not moisture tolerant.

Epoxy coatings produce the hardest surface. Water-based epoxies provide a clear finish and bond well to concrete, but depending on the solids content, they usually are nonporous and do not allow moisture in the slab to escape. Epoxies also come pigmented or tinted, but these products generally would not be used over a chemically stained floor. Be aware that epoxies require the surface to be profiled via acid etching or mechanical abrasion to give them something to adhere to. In most cases, however, you will obtain the necessary surface profile during the cleaning phase of the project and the application of the chemical stain itself,

due to its etching properties. Check the epoxy manufacturer's recommendations for obtaining a good bond.

Sealer application methods

The basic tool for applying sealer is a roller, supplemented by paintbrushes or paint pads to cut the sealer into tight corners.

Rollers come in a variety of types and nap thicknesses. Preferably, use a roller that is lint free. If you can't find one, try this simple trick used by many applicators: Run a layer of tape over the entire surface of the roller, and then peel the tape off. This removes any loose lint that would otherwise end up on the floor. Also read the label on the roller to verify what types of materials it can apply, such as oil- or water-based products, epoxies, or urethanes.

The roller nap thickness you choose depends on the texture of the concrete surface. For smooth, nontextured concrete, use a roller with a 3/16 to 1/4 inch nap. On textured concrete, a thicker 3/8 inch nap often works best.

Water- or solvent-based acrylic sealers and urethane sealers can usually be applied by simply dipping the roller into the sealer (contained either in a bucket or roller tray) and rolling the sealer onto the floor. Acrylic sealers can also be spray applied with a hand pump sprayer, high-volume low-pressure (HVLP) sprayer, or airless sprayer. The problem with an airless sprayer is that

The basic tool for applying most sealers is a lint-free roller. The nap thickness you choose depends on the texture of the concrete surface. For smooth, nontextured concrete, use a roller with a 3/16 to 1/4 inch nap. A thicker nap may be required for textured surfaces.

A coat of clear sealer can dramatically enhance the appearance of chemically stained surfaces by adding a sheen (if desired) and bringing out the depth of color.

if the pressure is set too high, it atomizes the sealer and makes it airborne, creating a cloud of sealer that is unhealthy to breathe. What's more, this cloud of sealer can filter back down onto the floor and leave a layer of what appears to be dust. I still like to use a roller after spraying just to key, or push, the sealer into the surface of the concrete. Urethanes can be spray applied as well, but most manufacturers say that it is necessary to backroll.

To apply epoxy coatings, which tend to be thicker than the other types, a notched squeegee rake can be used, depending on the mil thickness being put down. But you will still need to backroll behind the notched squeegee with a roller.

Applying the floor finish

The next step is to apply the floor finish, or wax. This sacrificial coating protects the sealer from wear.

The most commonly used type of floor finish is a mop-down product that can be applied with a looped-end rayon mop or a finish mop kit for applying floor finishes. Edges can be cut in with a sponge or rag. Never use a cotton mop to put down the floor finish because it will leave streaks. Use cotton mops only to clean the floor.

The majority of floor finishes are water-based acrylic copolymers designed for a specific use. There are also solvent-based

waxes that are applied with a heavy-duty floor machine equipped with different brush or buffing attachments. These products have exceptional resistance to scuffs and black heel marks. When properly maintained, they are also slip resistant. You can purchase most floor finish products from a janitorial supply house or from chemical stain manufacturers.

Most installers protect a stained concrete floor with a minimum of six coats of floor finish (if not as many as ten) before turning the floor over to the owner or owner's representative. The logic is this: The sacrificial wax coating not only makes the floor look nice, but also is a shock absorber to scuffs, scratches, and grime. It is very easy to buff out a coat of floor finish and then reapply more if necessary.

After these original applications of floor finish, the stained concrete surface should last indefinitely—as long as the owner is diligent about ongoing maintenance. The finish should never be allowed to wear down to the sealer because sealers are not as receptive as a floor finish to the buffing out of scratches and scuffs.

Tip

Check with the sealer manufacturer to ensure compatibility of the floor finish over specific sealers. Manufacturers of some sealers, such as chemical-resistant urethanes, do not recommend applying wax or a floor finish.

CHAPTER 17

EQUIPMENT, TOOLS, AND SUPPLIES

My students often ask about the initial upfront investment they must make in equipment, tools, and supplies to get started chemically staining interior concrete floors. I suggest starting with the essentials, and then adding items as the need arises and the budget allows.

The Basics

Of course, you will need the appropriate stains, dyes, grout, sealer, and floor finish (wax) for the job you're doing. Add to that these other "essential" items, which should total less than $1,000.

Basic Supplies	
Diamond blades for angle grinder	Spray bottles (various sizes) **
Orange or florescent chalk	Plastic containers to keep the stain in**
Watercolor pencils	Painter's tape (green or blue)
Rags	Masking plastic
Rayon mop head (looped end)	Duct tape (do not use on the concrete)
Cotton mop head	Non-absorbent vessels to contain stain drips
Mop bucket	Acid brushes
Plastic booties	Sponges
Commercially sold detergent (nonfilm forming, citrus based)	Trisodium phosphate (TSP) or muriatic acid (for cleaning spills)
Brooms (push broom or household broom to remove heavy dust or contaminants)	Ammonia or baking soda for neutralizing stain residue (or use prepackaged neutralizing packs)
Brushes (various sizes)*	Caution tape (to barricade work areas)

Basic Tools & Equipment

Wet/dry shop vacuum	Tape measure
4 inch angle grinder	Extension cords
Chalk line	Roller cages, heads, and handles
Water hose	1 or 2 gallon acid-resistant sprayer **
Scraper	Hand pump sprayer**

* Brushes should have acid-resistant, uncolored bristles. Sizes from 1/8 inch artist brushes up to 6 inch brushes (for borders) can be used.

**Supplies and tools that come into contact with chemical stains must resist hydrochloric acid.

Supplemental tools

As your needs and experience level expand, consider investing in the following products. Some equipment and tools, particularly for surface preparation where larger equipment may be needed, are good candidates for renting as the need arises. You can put the rental fee in the bid price, without having to store or maintain this equipment. Each contractor must develop parameters for when it makes sense to own versus rent.

Supplemental Supplies	Supplemental Tools & Equipment
Sanding pads and screens	Squeegee vacuum
Sea sponges	Rotary buffing machine
Eyedropper	Backpack pump sprayer
Tek Gel for etching (gelled acid)*	Saw cart and engraving tools for sawcutting pattern lines
Diamond bits for the Dremel tool	

* Available from Surface Gel Tek (www.surfacegeltek.com).

For less than $1,000, you can purchase all the basic supplies needed to stain concrete floors, including application tools, sprayers, cleaning supplies, masking materials, extension cords, marking chalk, and more.

LARRY BRAZIL PHOTOGRAPHY

A 1 or 2 gallon pump sprayer (left) and hand spray bottle (right) are most commonly used for stain application. Make sure all sprayer components are plastic; the hydrochloric acid in stain can react with metal.

LARRY BRAZIL PHOTOGRAPHY

Safety essentials

Finally, do not neglect getting personal protective gear for you and your crew. Items needed include:
• Hydrogen-chloride respirator
• Splash-resistant goggles
• Impervious gloves
• Protective clothing
• Dust respirator, safety glasses, and ear protection (when using power equipment)

Please refer back to Chapter 11 for more information on safety.

About diamond bits and blades

Diamond or carbide bits are commonly used for the Dremel tool. Keep in mind that the Dremel, in most cases, is used for short rather than long cuts. The bits, whether diamond or carbide, wear more quickly, especially on hard concrete surfaces. They can be used more successfully on some polymer-modified overlay systems, due to the fact that these systems contain smaller aggregates. For 98% of your sawcuts, you will use a grinder or saw-cutting equipment. The Dremel is a complementary companion.

Diamond blades come in a variety of shapes and sizes. The most popular diamond blades are either segmented or continuous rim. Most stain artisans prefer a continuous-rimmed blade because more surface area comes in contact with the substrate during cutting. Also, different regions have harder aggregates in their concrete mixes. As a general rule, use a hard-bonded diamond blade to cut green concrete and a soft-bonded diamond blade to cut harder concrete surfaces. Regardless of the blade you choose, it is a good idea to make some pilot cuts on a separate surface from the slab, such as a cinder block or old piece of concrete, to take the hard edge off the blade before you cut the slab.

For elaborate stained designs, such as the one shown above,
keep on hand eyedroppers and brushes of various sizes,
from 1/8 inch artist brushes to 6 inch brushes for borders (inset).

For detail work, keep on hand eyedroppers and
brushes of various sizes, from 1/8 inch artist brushes
to 6 inch brushes for borders.

CHAPTER 18

SPECIALTY TECHNIQUES

Basic one-coat stain applications with sealer and multi-coat stain applications with decorative sawcuts form the largest percentage of chemical staining projects. However, a growing number of clients opt for something more when they see the design possibilities achievable with various specialty techniques.

Personalizing floors with company logos or creative artwork, using dyes to extend the color palette, using faux finishing techniques, or applying chemicals that leave intriguing effects are just several of many ways to further enhance stained concrete floor designs. In addition, the use of materials that "resist" the chemical stain, preventing it from penetrating and reacting, can produce unusual shapes and outlines.

With some imagination and skill, concrete artisans can broaden their horizons and take their work to the next level. The table on pages 76-77 describes some of the techniques used to create one-of-a-kind concrete flooring.

GERALD TAYLOR

Using dyes to extend the color palette, faux finishing, and other specialty techniques, concrete artisans can take their work to the next level.

Unique effects can be achieved with very simple items, some of which can be found around the house. Torn paper, cheesecloth, and sponges can double as application tools. Metal shavings and fertilizer pellets react with stain, creating interesting color variations. And gelled acid can be used with decorative stencils to produce precisely etched patterns.

The delicate look of fern fronds can be achieved by applying stain in a sawcut then "blowing" the stain across the surface using compressed air. Start by cutting the stem lines into the concrete freehand using a 4 inch angle grinder. Next, use an eyedropper to fill the cuts with stain. Finally, use the air tool fitted with a fine tip to gently blow the stain onto the surface as desired

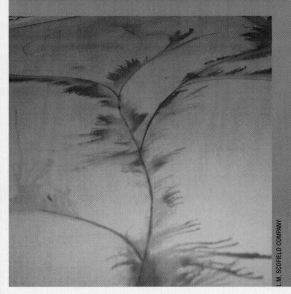

Concrete dyes	When concrete dyes are combined with chemical staining, there are no limitations from a predetermined color palette or color values. Some artisans consider concrete dyes to be a companion on many chemical stain jobs for a variety of reasons. Dyes can produce bright, vibrant colors such as yellows and blues, and applicators have the ability to mix their own custom colors. Dyes can also soften areas where the chemical stain has produced an overly bright tone. Or they can enhance stain colors in areas of the slab where the stain is not reacting with the concrete and the color needs to be enhanced. For more information on using dyes, see Chapter 15.
Decorative sandblasting	Intriguing effects are possible by sandblasting after staining, particularly when decorative stencils are used. The stencils are applied to the concrete surface before sandblasting, so only the areas not covered by the stencils are revealed. After the stencils are removed, the protected areas can be stained or dyed a contrasting color. Manufacturers sell decorative stencils that are sandblast resistant and adhesive backed. Different degrees of tack on the back are available, so choose carefully. A high-tack backing could lift the sealer from the substrate or, in warm conditions, transfer mastic to the surface, which could be difficult to remove later. Conversely, a light-tack adhesive in cool conditions may not adhere aggressively enough. For this reason, most manufacturers recommend a coat of sealer prior to sandblasting to improve stencil adhesion. Some stencil suppliers can custom cut logos or other patterns using a computer-guided plotter. This enables you to have precision-cut stencils without the hassle or time of cutting them yourself. In most cases, all you need to provide is good-quality artwork. Some companies also have stock designs you can choose from.
Faux finishes	The same techniques and tools that have been used for years to faux finish walls can also be used on concrete flooring. Application tools include rags, torn paper, plastic, and sea sponges to name a few.
Applying a resist	A resist is anything that impedes the stain from penetrating into the surface of the concrete substrate. Sealer is often used as a resist, especially on projects with intricate sawcut patterns. Once the appropriate amount of sealer has been put down and has had sufficient dry time, it forms a barrier that blocks the stain or other liquids from penetrating the concrete surface. With some creativity and experience using sealer as a resist, you can stretch your imagination. For example, incorporate "veins" into floor designs by applying sealer with an eyedropper or artist's brush prior to staining. Other application tools include crumpled rags, sea sponges, and goose feathers. Keep in mind that not all sealers are equal, and a test panel should be conducted to check the suitability of the resist. Another way to resist the stain from penetrating designated areas is with masking plastic. However, this method is generally not practical for masking off detailed sawcut patterns.
Sealer	In addition to being used as a resist, sealers can add the final touch to a stained concrete project by enhancing the colors you have worked so hard to achieve. You can also choose from various degrees of sheen, ranging from matte to high-gloss.

Gelled-acid etching	Tek Gel* for etching can be used with decorative stencils in a manner similar to decorative sandblasting. Tek Gel contains acid, which is responsible for its etching ability, but the acid is suspended in a gel solution so its interaction with the concrete is limited to the surface. Because of the product's gelatinous grip, it stays on the stencil and won't bleed underneath it, etching only the exposed areas to produce a very precisely etched pattern. The product also will not compromise the pH of the concrete, and it will not contaminate the sewage system after it is flushed.
Engraving	The KaleidoCrete system** cuts intricate or one-of-a-kind designs into concrete. It uses an assortment of engraving tools guided by templates, which are available in thousands of patterns and designs, including letters, logos, borders, and custom graphics. The tools can also be used freehand. The main component of the KaleidoCrete system is the Shark Concrete Engraver. This handheld driver powers 64 sharpened and heat-treated impactor teeth that leave a detailed cut up to 1/4 inch deep. The operator controls the precision and depth of cut. The Mongoose, a small wheel-mounted decorative concrete engraving saw, can be used to do engraving work in small or restricted areas. When equipped with an optional center pivot, it can also cut perfect circles. The Wasp, often called a "concrete pencil" because it can be used freehand to engrave letters into concrete, is handy for doing touchup work after the Shark and for adding fine details.
Fertilizer	The iron and nitrogen in fertilizers, such as Miracle Grow, dissolve and leave unique etchings on the concrete floor. One of the more popular techniques is to use fertilizer pellets. Usually the pellets are applied to the concrete surface prior to staining. However, some artisans will first apply a base color of stain and then apply the fertilizer pellets followed by a second color of stain to achieve different effects.
Sawdust, kitty litter, and other absorbent materials	Sawdust and kitty litter applied to the concrete surface during staining will absorb the stain and leave an outline on the concrete floor. As with fertilizer pellets, sawdust or kitty litter can be applied at different phases of the project to create different effects. Sampling is essential to achieving the exact look you are after. Other common absorbent materials used to create special effects include corn flakes and metal shavings. The creative possibilities are unlimited when you use some of these materials combined with staining.
Torn paper, torn edges of rags	Torn paper, torn rags, or any item with a ragged edge can be used to transfer the look of a vein or cracked edge onto the floor. Stain or dye can be sprayed across the edge of the torn paper to achieve this effect. Or rags (torn into strips) can be applied to the concrete surface and then stained to create the look of a crack.
Air	Accents can be created by "blowing" the stain across the surface, using compressed air forced through a fine tip. For example, by applying stain with an eyedropper into the channel of a decorative sawcut, and then using the air tool to blow the stain out, you can achieve the delicate look of vines or ferns. Be aware that while using air, some of the stain can become airborne. It is essential to wear protective gear and safety glasses or goggles when using this technique.

*Available from Surface Gel Tek (www.surfacegeltek.com).
**Available from Engrave-A-Crete (www.engraveacrete.com).

Faux "cracks" in stained surfaces
can also be painted on with
an artist's brush, using a darker shade
of stain than the base color.

The Shark engraver and Wasp concrete pencil
were used to create this custom logo for
a coffee company. A reusable stencil served
as the cutting guide for the engraving tools.

Applying stain with an eyedropper over aluminum shavings results in a chemical reaction that intensifies the color around the shavings. After the reaction, simply sweep the shavings away.

To achieve a marbleized look in small sections, apply the stain in a random manner with an eyedropper.

A simple faux finishing technique is to dab the stain onto the surface with a rag, producing a mottled effect.

This design was achieved with decorative stencils and sandblasting. The stencil is applied to the floor after chemical staining, and then the surface is sandblasted to reveal only the areas not covered by the stencil.

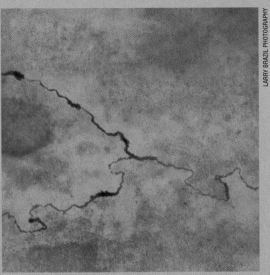

Torn paper, rags, or any item with a ragged edge can be used to transfer the look of a vein or cracked edge onto the floor.

The iron and nitrogen in fertilizer pellets dissolve and leave unique etchings on the concrete floor. Usually the pellets are applied to the surface prior to staining. However, here the artisan applied the fertilizer pellets over a base color of stain and then added a darker color of stain for variation.

This striking medallion incorporates a variety of special staining techniques. "Veining" was used in the black sections, a technique that involves applying sealer with an eyedropper or artist's brush prior to staining to act as a resist. In the four corners, a patina effect was achieved by applying fertilizer pellets.

L.M. SCOFIELD COMPANY

81

Taking extra precautions throughout the project will help to reduce the number of problems that arise. The above work area has been masked off in an effort to keep other workers on the job off the floor.

CHAPTER 19

TROUBLESHOOTING: HOW TO FIX COMMON FIELD PROBLEMS

Even if you prepare field samples in advance using the same stains and techniques you plan to use on the floor, things can still go awry once the project gets underway. In many cases, taking immediate action can prevent minor accidents, such as stain drips, from turning into major headaches. But if you are unable to attack the problem right away, there are still techniques you can use to cover up or repair unsightly problem areas.

Of course, the best strategy is to prevent such mishaps from occurring in the first place. So this chapter also discusses some measures to take to avoid common problems.

Remove chemical stain spills from concrete surfaces

To remove accidental stain spills, use a solution of trisodium phosphate (TSP) and water. Try to rinse the spill immediately, before the stain has time to react and fully absorb into the surface. By rubbing the spill firmly with a rag, you should be able to erase most of the mark.

On highly absorbent surfaces, it may be impossible to fully remove the spill, but with some care you can soften or mask it substantially. On small areas, a good trick is to scrape the surface gently with the sharp edge of a utility knife or margin trowel to remove most of the spill, and then rub the concrete powder removed from the floor back into the affected area to soften the remaining stain.

If you are trying to remove a stain spill that has had time to react with and absorb into the concrete surface, a more aggressive approach may be required. In many cases, the best eraser will be diluted muriatic acid. Predampen the affected area, and then rub the spill with a diluted acid solution. Start with a dilution that is not overly aggressive, such as 15 parts water to 1 part muriatic acid. If this solution does not do the trick, it may be necessary to increase the amount of muriatic acid to make the solution stronger. Whatever the strength of the acid solution used, apply it by rubbing and dabbing the area with the tip of a rag as opposed to letting the solution just sit on the surface.

Two other methods to consider for removing stain spills are applying gelled acid or lightly sanding the surface. Gelled acid (described in Chapter 18) can be effective providing that you closely monitor the degree of etching. Try light sanding only if you can do so without scratching the surface. Some skim coats or overlays can withstand sanding without scratching.

With some skill and patience, you should be able to get the results you need with one of these methods. However, it may not be necessary to remove all spills or drips if you intend to go back over the problem area with a darker stain color. Generally, applying darker stain will mask the spill.

A keen attention to detail is the first step in producing gorgeous floors such as this entryway.

Take these measures to avoid common problems

• Never use a high-build tape, like duct tape or yellow fabric tape, to mask off the floor because it could leave mastic residue that will resist the stain. Only use green or blue painter's tape.

• Inspect the masking plastic closely prior to staining. Put a piece of tape on any tears or small holes that the stain can work its way through.

• Before applying stain with a sprayer, test the sprayer with water to make sure a steady stream is coming out of the tip. Splatter can be caused from a lack of sufficient air pumped into the sprayer or from a clogged tip. It is also a good idea to have a backup sprayer on the job ready to go without delay.

• Take extreme care during the sawcutting phase of the project to avoid overcuts that will need to be patched later.

• Be extremely careful not to track stain onto unmasked areas when walking around the project. It is inevitable that the bottom of your shoes will pick up any stain that collects on top of the masking plastic during the spraying process. One solution is to wear slip-on booties over your shoes.

• When possible, apply the lightest stain colors on the project first so if there is any overspray or the stain gets through tears in the masking plastic, the darker stain colors will cover up the problem.

• Always maintain a wet edge while applying chemical stains. If the chemical staining process stops in the middle of the floor and the application restarts later, a distinguishable line may result. (See Chapter 14 for more advice on avoiding stain lines.)

• Always place a nonabsorbent vessel under the container holding the stain to collect any drips that run down the side of the container. These drips can leave a ring on the floor.

• To avoid a distinguishable spray pattern, use a conical tip rather than a fan spray to apply the stain.

• Take precautions when removing the masking plastic after staining. If there is stain on top of the plastic, it can splatter and contaminate adjoining areas. Prevent drips by carefully rolling the plastic into a ball and putting it into a bucket for disposal rather than carrying the ball of plastic across the floor.

• When cleaning the slab after stain application, use the "white glove" test (described in Chapter 14) to make sure that all residue has been lifted from the surface.

• Before applying sealer, make sure no standing moisture is in the sawcut and the edge of the cut is not darker than the surrounding area. In most cases, once the slab is sealed those areas will retain the moisture and remain darkened indefinitely. Use a heat gun, blow dryer, or leaf blower to dry out these areas.

Cover up spray splatter

If during the staining process spray splatter occurs due to a clogged tip or lack of pressure in the sprayer, get the sprayer out of production immediately and switch to your backup sprayer. Spray a topcoat over the splattered area as soon as possible, before the splatter reacts and dries. A second coat of stain can help hide splattered areas as well.

Remove drywall mud, paint, or caulk

In most cases, removing drywall plaster is more of an annoyance than a problem. First, use a floor scraper to scrape off the bulk of the material. Then use cold or warm water along with a rotary floor buffer with a black scouring pad or sanding screen to remove the remaining drywall residue.

If paint spills are on the floor, a floor scraper is again your best weapon for removing the paint. Use paint thinner to remove any paint that remains after scraping.

Scraping should also remove most caulk residue. But in extreme cases, you may need to apply a poultice saturated with denatured alcohol, as described in Chapter 12.

Concrete surface absorbs stain too quickly

If you notice that the stain is being absorbed too quickly because the surface is highly porous, then it may be necessary to prewet the surface to obtain a saturated surface dry (SSD) condition. Apply water onto the surface by misting. Once the water has evaporated, the staining process can start.

Prewetting the surface, which also cools down the slab, slows both the absorption and reaction of the stain so brush strokes or spray lines do not show as much as they would when stain is applied to warm or porous surfaces. However, be careful not to leave excess moisture in sawcuts or joints.

Remove blue or red chalk that has been lacquered down

Throughout this guide, I have recommended the use of light or fluorescent chalk because the iron oxide in blue and red chalk can permanently stain a concrete surface. Blue and red chalk become increasingly problematic if you spray lacquer over the top of the chalk line to prevent water from washing it away during the sawcutting process. If this scenario occurs, a solvent such as xylene or lacquer thinner may be needed to remove most of the lacquer followed by a rotary floor scrubber with a black pad or sanding screen. Always do a moisture absorbency check with water prior to staining to make sure that the lacquer was completely removed.

Patch an overcut from sawcutting

To repair an overcut, use a patch made with the same concrete materials used in the substrate. If the overcut is in conventional ready-mixed concrete, sand, cement, and a little bit of polymer as a bonding agent can generally be used to make the repair. Prepackaged anchoring cement also works well and will take the stain. If the overcut is in an overlay, such as a stampable or self-leveling product, use the same overlay material to make the repair.

Erase brush strokes from stained surfaces

A second coat of stain can soften brush strokes left from the first coat. On highly absorbent surfaces, brush strokes and spray lines may be clearly evident after the first coat of stain. A second coat of stain will generally cover up these marks.

A softer effect is desired

Diluting stain will usually produce a softer look. Sometimes you can build up the color in stages to achieve the desired look. For more on diluting stains, see Chapter 14.

The stain did not take or the stain is blotchy

Consider applying a second coat of stain in areas where the stain did not take and the floor has a blotchy appearance, almost like leopard skin. Spot staining these problematic areas can help the floor look more uniform.

Dyes can also enhance stain colors in areas of the slab where the stain is not reacting to the concrete and the color needs to be enhanced.

Inspect the masking plastic closely prior to staining. If you find a tear or small hole (top), cover it with tape so no stain can get through during application (bottom).

CHAPTER 20

MAINTAINING CHEMICALLY STAINED FLOORS

After the original applications of floor finish (wax) at the end of the chemical staining project, the stained concrete floor should last for many years to come—as long as the owner is vigilant about ongoing maintenance.

Concrete that is not properly sealed and waxed can become soiled and contaminated quickly. That is why it is important to encourage the owner to implement a maintenance schedule that best suits the floor's needs.

How much care is needed?

The key factors dictating the amount of ongoing maintenance required are the amount of traffic the floor receives and the type of sealer used. Generally, the floor finish is applied to preserve the sealer that is protecting the stained work. The floor finish should never be allowed to wear down to the sealer because a sealer is not as easy to maintain as a floor finish. The beauty of starting off with the appropriate amount of floor finish (typically six to ten coats) after you have applied the last coat of sealer is that it will make the floor easier to maintain throughout its life. Floor finish can be applied with a looped-end or finish mop with relative ease.

In most cases, residential concrete floors experience light foot traffic. Periodic maintenance is minimal if the appropriate amount of floor finish is applied early on. Frequent wet mopping or dry dust mopping of the floor is normally the only regular maintenance needed. If the floor loses its brilliant luster or shine, cleaning of the floor and a coat or two of floor finish will bring it back to its original state. In a non-aggressive environment such as a

home, it is not uncommon to have a year or more go by with just light maintenance before it is necessary to buff and rewax the floor. We like to factor into our bid several gallons of additional wax, over and above what was applied to the floor originally. If clients have the wax on hand, they are more likely to use it when needed as opposed to trying to find a source where they can purchase it.

In a moderately aggressive environment, such as a restaurant, floor maintenance might entail going in at night once a month to reapply the floor finish. The finish is applied to act as a shock absorber for the sealer, taking the brunt of all of the scratches and scuffs. These blemishes can generally be buffed out and then filled with another layer or two of wax.

In a very aggressive environment, such as a shopping mall where foot traffic is heavy and continual, floor maintenance may be required as often as two or three times per month. Depending on the size of the floor and frequency of maintenance, it may be more cost effective for your client to hire a professional floor care company to maintain the floor. Companies in the business of floor maintenance have the necessary equipment to strip and reapply wax in a timely fashion in a large commercial environment. Also, they can use a high-speed burnishing machine to achieve an exceptionally high gloss.

A very simple way to determine maintenance frequency is to look at a floor and see if it is losing its sheen and if there are excessive scuffs and scratches. If so, more frequent maintenance may be needed. By educating your clients about this straightforward approach, they can protect their investment for many years to come.

Know the type of sealer used

The type of sealer used on stained concrete flooring will also play a role in the maintenance required and the life of the floor. With so many different sealer options available in the market, it is imperative to check manufacturer recommendations for application and proper coverage rates when considering which sealer will best suit your needs. Some manufacturers suggest that it is acceptable to wax over a urethane, while others caution against applying wax on some industrial polyurethanes such as chemical-resistant urethanes (CRUs). Because of the impermeability of CRUs, the floor finish may not adhere properly.

Always check the manufacturer's recommendations for floor care. Think of the sealer and the maintenance of the floor as a system.

Chemically stained floors are easy to maintain when protected with several coats of floor finish. Put the finish down with a looped-end rayon mop after the final coat of sealer dries.

Reduce wear and tear with floor mats

Another part of a maintenance plan, especially in an aggressive environment such as a restaurant or shopping mall with heavy foot traffic, is to use floor mats both inside and outside of the building.

When people walk across an asphalt or a concrete parking lot, their shoes pick up sand and grit. A mat outside will knock most of this debris off their shoes. Including another floor mat inside the building will trap even more grit. Thus simple floor mats can help preserve the floor by reducing the amount of grime being ground into the floor finish. When excessive sand or grit is on the floor over a period of time, the life of the floor is significantly reduced. Under repeated foot traffic, this grit acts like sandpaper by wearing away the floor finish and sealer much more quickly.

CHAPTER 21

HOW TO SELL CHEMICALLY STAINED INTERIOR FLOORS

Even the finest and most experienced craftsman needs to get the word out about his business. Some contractors who produce fabulous interior floors believe the work should sell itself and that no energy should be spent promoting their business. More often than not, this is just not true. In fact, sometimes contractors with lesser ability will go farther in business because they promote and market their services more effectively.

Listed in this chapter are what I consider the fundamentals to selling chemically stained interior concrete floors.

Do phenomenal work

Our company did an interior floor at a day spa near our hometown of Temple, Georgia. We constantly receive inquiries from people who see our work there. Each job should be looked at as a calling card for your company.

Continually hone your craft

There should be continual improvement in your product as each year passes. Network with others to expand your knowledge. In the decorative concrete business, there is always more to learn no matter what your skill level.

Concentrate your marketing efforts

Use the rifle approach, rather than the shotgun approach, to selling. General contractors, architects, builders, and designers will award you repeat work if you do a great job for them. A large percentage of your personal selling and other marketing efforts should be directed at this group. A great relationship with several builders can deliver a large amount of business to your firm.

Make an impression with professional samples and a portfolio

Carrying sample boards with you is an effective way of showing your work.

Keep a portfolio with good photography showing your interior floors. At some point, consider a showroom where prospects can see colors and patterns. A showroom might simply be in the lobby of your office or it could be a conference room in your office large enough to host groups of architects or other design professionals. Always keep a database of past successful jobs to refer people to.

Utilize your supplier network

Your chemical stain supplier, rental equipment yard, and ready-mix suppliers can all be good sources of referrals. Keep this important group informed of interesting projects you have done—particularly jobs where you have used their materials or equipment. Drop off pictures of your work to your suppliers occasionally so they can see what you are capable of doing.

Deliver excellent customer service

Return phone calls, fix your mistakes, dress professionally, be proactive, and anticipate issues: These are the little things that are going to set your firm apart from the competition. Earning a reputation for excellent work and reliability will serve you well.

Consider setting up a showroom in your office to display samples of what you can accomplish to architects, design professionals, and other prospective clients.

Establish a professional web site

A web site helps introduce new prospects to your firm and helps new or existing clients learn more about your capabilities in a nonthreatening manner. A web site can also save you extensive amounts of time by allowing prospective customers to review your colors, designs, and portfolio before you even meet them in person.

Contribute design ideas

Rarely are specifications for chemically stained interior floors clear-cut, even on commercial projects. In most cases, owners, designers, builders, and architects will welcome your design ideas and suggestions. For many contractors, their favorite jobs are those where they have input in personalizing the floor with the designer and owner. Blood, sweat, and talent by themselves do not make an awesome floor; vision does.

Having an artistic vision will work to your advantage. However, if you are not the artistic type, refer back to Chapter 3 for some good sources of design ideas.

Be patient

Becoming proficient at chemical staining does not happen overnight. Likewise, building a business on a solid foundation takes time. Decide early on in the life of your business if you have the motivation and desire to build a business the right way—slow and steady.

It takes many years to be an overnight success!

CHAPTER 22

THE FUTURE: ARTISANS TAKING STAINED FLOORS OVER THE TOP

The backgrounds of the contractors who produce beautiful interior concrete floors are as varied as the palette of colors they work from. Mike Miller was a salesman for a concrete stain manufacturer, Dave Pettigrew a journeyman carpenter, and Dana Boyer an artist by trade. Each of these talented artisans brings their own inspiration to each project.

Mike Miller – The Concretist
(www.theconcretist.com)

For Mike Miller, president and managing principal of The Concretist Inc., Mother Nature played a unique role in piquing his interest in concrete. Back when he was selling concrete stain, Miller visited Yosemite National Park for a job and had the chance to explore the Ahwahnee Hotel.

Completed in 1927, the Ahwahnee features a unique blend of design influences including Art Deco, Native American, Middle Eastern, and the Arts and Crafts Movement. These elements can be seen in every aspect of the hotel, including stenciling, woodwork, lighting fixtures, and china patterns. But what struck Miller most was the stained concrete, which he calls "one of the great (concrete) wonders of the world."

Known in the industry for reshaping attitudes about chemical stains, Miller experiments with new ways to use the materials and preaches the value of finishes that reveal wide color ranges and subtle variations. The first large commercial project to be recognized for this approach was The Forum Shops at Caesars Palace in Las Vegas.

One of Miller's goals is to always give concrete a voice, which he does by utilizing his senses. In fact, his Benicia, California-based company is an association of independent artists, craftsmen, and others who specialize in producing "sensory" concrete art and architecture. First, Miller takes a close look at the concrete—searching for qualities that may not be apparent at first glance, such as aggregate near the surface. Then he listens to his clients to hear what is important to them. Finally, there is intuition. Miller says that you have to see things that most people can't.

Miller also acknowledges that concrete is an imperfect material: The harder you try to make it consistent, the less success you will have. Instead, he takes advantage of the imperfections and uses them to make the work interesting.

Dave Pettigrew – Diamond D Concrete
(www.diamonddcompany.com)

A former journeyman carpenter and now owner of Diamond D Company, Watsonville, California, David Pettigrew knows all about the 4 Cs—and they do not have anything to do with diamonds. They stand for concrete, concrete, concrete, and concrete: colored, stained, stamped, and engraved.

When Pettigrew was a kid, he loved to draw all kinds of artistic designs, primarily interesting geometric shapes, which he would color in and then use to cover his textbooks. Today, he has applied this passion to concrete, creating unique, brilliant pieces of art on floors, driveways, and countertops—anything made of concrete. Pettigrew says that he has always loved this "miracle material" because it can be molded into any shape the artist desires. His exquisite concrete floors have been awarded Bomanite Gold Awards for Residential Patene Artectura.

Pettigrew says his favorite project of all time is the La Honda house. He was basically given free reign on the project, and designed the various rooms of the house along with a friend. The kitchen is graced with beautiful mahogany-colored concrete countertops. The kitchen floor resembles a stunning piece of artwork, resplendent in rich hues of amber, gold, and sage thoughtfully arranged in interesting, interlocking shapes. A swath of the brown color matching the countertops accentuates the floor design. Pettigrew notes that everyone who comes into the house can't believe it's concrete.

Pettigrew gets calls from people as far away as Australia, Great Britain, and Canada, many asking his secret to achieving such dazzling colors. Pettigrew has indeed mastered the coloring process, achieving rich vibrant hues in a range of colors. But he calls the learning curve "brutal." And on many projects, his stomach does "flip-flops" as he waits to make sure the results come out all right.

The Concretist

Diamond D Concrete

ConcretiZen

Dana Boyer – ConcretiZen
(www.concretizen.com)

An artist by trade, Dana Boyer spent years as a painter, creating unique custom and airbrush designs for myriad surfaces, including automobiles. She also worked professionally on a wide range of faux painting projects. Several years ago, she wanted to paint her own concrete floor and turned to concrete experts for advice and quick training. She has been using concrete as her medium ever since.

Boyer began working with The Concretist's Mike Miller, experimenting with new ways to use chemical stains. Now, as owner of ConcretiZen, based in Apache Junction, Arizona, she has gone beyond staining to provide a variety of residential and commercial services, including overlays, stucco staining, resurfacing, polishing, sandblasting, stamping, texturing, and engraving. She has traveled all over the country to do everything from stamped countertops in Napa Valley to unique floors in Pennsylvania.

What Boyer loves about concrete are the unlimited possibilities—the work continues to inspire her over and over again. She says that just when she does something she thinks she can't top, she will do something else and feel the same way.

Boyer affirms that the market for concrete is really beginning to grow. The industry, she says, is definitely headed in a "new direction." Many people are now looking at concrete as a real option as they rip out their floors and carpeting.

GLOSSARY

A

absorption – The process by which a liquid is drawn into and tends to fill permeable pores in a porous solid body, such as concrete.

accelerator – An admixture used to shorten the set time of concrete and/or speed strength development.

admixture – A material other than water, cement, and aggregate used to modify the properties of concrete in its freshly mixed, setting, or hardened states.

aggregate – A granular material such as crushed stone, sand, or gravel used with a cementing medium (such as portland cement) to form concrete or mortar.

air-entraining admixture – Added to fresh concrete to cause the development of a system of microscopic air bubbles. Helps to improve the workability of fresh concrete and the freeze/thaw resistance of hardened concrete.

B

broom finish – Surface texture obtained by pushing a broom over freshly placed concrete.

C

calcium chloride vapor-emission test – A test used to measure the volume of water vapor radiating from a concrete substrate over time (typically 24 hours). The amount of moisture emitted from a slab can affect stain color and sealer performance.

cement (portland) – A hydraulic product that sets and hardens when it chemically interacts with water. Made by burning a mixture of limestone and clay or similar materials.

coarse aggregate – Graded granular material with a nominal maximum size ranging from 3/8 inch to 1 1/2 inches.

concrete – A composite material consisting essentially of a binding medium within which aggregate particles are embedded. In portland-cement concrete, the binder is formed from a mixture of portland cement and water.

curing – Action taken to maintain moisture and temperature conditions of freshly placed concrete during a defined period of time following placement. Helps to ensure adequate hydration of the cementitious materials and proper hardening of the concrete.

curing compound – A liquid that, when applied to the surface of newly placed concrete, forms a membrane that retards the evaporation of water.

E

efflorescence – A deposit of salts that forms on a concrete surface, usually as a whitish powder or crust.

F

fine aggregate – A graded granular material entirely passing the 3/8 inch sieve.

float finish – Surface texture (usually rough) obtained by finishing with a float.

fly ash – A pozzolan resulting from the combustion of ground or powdered coal; sometimes used in concrete as a partial replacement for portland cement.

G

granulated blast-furnace slag – A glassy, granular material formed when molten blast-furnace slag is rapidly chilled. Sometimes used in concrete mixtures as a partial replacement for portland cement to help reduce permeability and improve durability.

grout – A cementitious mixture, with or without admixtures, used primarily to fill voids.

H

hard-troweled finish – Surface finish obtained by using a trowel with a steel blade (either handheld or power) for final finishing of concrete. Often used on indoor slabs where a smooth, hard, flat surface is desired.

J

joint (contraction, expansion, or isolation) – Formed, sawed, or tooled groove in a concrete slab used to regulate the location of cracking (contraction joint) or to allow expansion or movement of adjoining structures.

M

mix design – Specific proportions of ingredients (cement, aggregates, water, and admixtures) used to produce concrete suited for a particular set of job conditions.

P

pozzolan – A siliceous or siliceous and aluminous material that, in the presence of moisture, chemically reacts with calcium hydroxide to form compounds possessing cementitious properties.

R

radiant floor heating – A system whereby warm water circulates through tubing embedded in a floor, turning the floor into an efficient, low-temperature radiator. Many radiant floor heating systems are embedded in slab-on-grade concrete because it offers a greater thermal mass than alternative flooring materials.

S

sand – Fine aggregate resulting from natural disintegration and abrasion of rock or processing of sandstone.

saturated surface dry (SSD) – Condition of concrete when the permeable voids are filled with water but no water is present on exposed surfaces.

sealer – Solvent- or liquid-based material used to protect and enhance the appearance of stained concrete or as a resist prior to staining to achieve special effects.

setting – The chemical reaction that occurs after the addition of water to a cementitious mixture, resulting in a gradual development of rigidity.

silicosis – A chronic disease of the lungs caused by the inhalation of silica dust over time. Silica is a chief mineral constituent of sand and many types of rock. Sandblasting, polishing, cutting, or grinding of concrete can release silica dust.

slump – A measure of consistency of freshly mixed concrete, as determined by the distance the concrete "slumps" after a molded specimen is removed from an inverted funnel-shaped cone.

W

water reducer – An admixture that increases the slump of freshly mixed concrete without increasing water content or maintains workability with a reduced amount of water.

workability –The ease of which freshly mixed concrete can be mixed, placed, compacted, and finished.

RESOURCES

Ready to get started with decorative concrete staining? Here are some good resources for tools, supplies, equipment, and training. Many of these companies will ship their products worldwide.

BRICKFORM RAFCO PRODUCTS

11061 Jersey Blvd.
Rancho Cucamonga, CA 91730
Phone: 800-483-9628
Fax: 909-484-3318
www.brickform.com

Offers a full line of decorative concrete products including acid stains, integral color, color hardener, overlays, sealers, sandblast stencils, and texture mats.

COLORMAKER FLOORS LTD.

2080 Enterprise Blvd.
West Sacramento, CA 95798
Phone: 888-875-9425
www.colormakerfloors.com

Offers a unique line of polished concrete toppings, cementitious overlays, concrete resurfacers, acid stains, dyes, integral coloring, and sealers exclusively for decorative concrete flooring applications.

CONCRETE IMPRESSIONS

P.O. Box 34406
San Antonio, TX 78265
Phone: 210-646-8500
Fax: 210-646-0556
www.concreteimpressions.com

Specializes in quality coloring systems for concrete, including acid stains, integral color, color hardener, and water-based tints for producing translucent hues. Other products include overlay systems, sealers, and cleaners and strippers specially formulated for concrete.

CONCRETE SOLUTIONS INC.

3904 Riley St.
San Diego, CA 92110
Phone: 800-232-8311
Fax: 619-297-3333
www.concretesolutions.com

Supplies products for the repair, restoration, and beautification of existing surfaces, such as a stampable overlay system, a spray-applied polymer-modified cement for recoloring or restoring concrete, and a decorative color-flake system for producing granite or terrazzo looks.

CONCRETENETWORK.COM, INC.

11375 Oak Hill Lane
Yucaipa, CA 92399
Phone: 866-380-7754
Fax: 909-389-7744
www.concretenetwork.com

The Concrete Network provides a window to the world of concrete products, concrete services, and concrete service providers. Visitors to the site can find information on many popular concrete topics, including decorative concrete floors, concrete countertops, decorative concrete pool decks, patios, driveways, and much more.

CROSSFIELD PRODUCTS

3000 E. Harcourt St.
Rancho Dominguez, CA 90221
Phone: 310-886-9100
Fax: 310-886-9119
www.miracote.com

Crossfield's Miracote decorative finishes for interior or exterior concrete are polymer-based and environmentally friendly. They can be used to achieve many different looks, from intricate, artistic designs to textured antique finishes. Also included in the product line are waterproofing systems, pigmentation products, coatings, and sealers.

DECORATIVE CONCRETE IMPRESSIONS

25067 Hawthorne Road
Webb City, MO 64870
Phone: 866-332-7383
Fax: 866-623-4793
www.decrete.com

Offers stencil patterns and borders, with over 30 designs in stock. Also available: color hardener, acid stains, and texture rollers and mats for producing natural stone or granite textures in decorative concrete.

DECORATIVE CONCRETE INSTITUTE

8729 South Flat Rock Road
Douglasville, GA 30134
Phone: 877-324-8080
Fax: 770-489-4948
www.decorativeconcreteinstitute.com

Bob Harris' Decorative Concrete Institute provides consulting, distribution of quality concrete products, education, installation, and on-the-job training to architects, artists, concrete finishers, faux finishers, general contractors, and interior designers across the U.S. and internationally. Some of the topics covered in the curriculum include proper surface and floor preparation, faux finishes, design layout, decorative score cutting, staining techniques, sandblasted and engraved graphics, stenciling, and stamping.

DECOSUP

8232 N.W. 56 St.
Miami, FL 33166
Phone: 305-468-9998
Fax: 305-468-9997
www.decosup.com

Ships decorative concrete products anywhere in the U.S. and the world. Choose from acid stains, dyes, decorative overlays, sealers, and more.

ENGRAVE-A-CRETE

Manasota Industrial Park
4693 19th Street Court East
Bradenton, FL 34203
Phone: 800-884-2114
Fax: 941-744-2600
www.engraveacrete.com

Provides tools to score, saw, engrave, or cut decorative designs in concrete, including the Mongoose, Wasp, and KaleidoCrete system. Many standard and custom template patterns also are available.

INTERNATIONAL SURFACE PREPARATION

6040 Osborn St.
Houston, TX 77054
Phone: 800-374-4043
Fax: 713-644-1785
www.surfacepreparation.com

Worldwide distributor of concrete cutting, grinding, and surface preparation equipment is the source for the Crac-Vac for decorative straight cutting, handheld and walk-behind grinders for profiling and mastic removal, and shotblasting equipment for surface preparation and profiling.

KEMIKO CONCRETE PRODUCTS

P.O. Box 1109
Leonard, TX 75452
Phone: 903-587-3708
Fax: 903-587-9038
www.kemiko.com

Kemiko's Stone Tone line of acid stains, wax, and sealer can be used to give concrete floors the look of marble or glazed stone. Also available: an acrylic-urethane polymer stain offered in a full palette of bold colors.

KEY RESIN COMPANY

4061 Clough Woods Drive
Batavia, OH 45103
Phone: 888-943-4532
www.keyresin.com

Specializes in epoxy resin systems for concrete. Products for decorative flooring applications include clear resin finishes combined with colored aggregates, thin-set terrazzo systems, and clear and colored protective coatings.

RESOURCES *continued*

L. M. SCOFIELD COMPANY

6533 Bandini Blvd.
Los Angeles, CA 90040
Phone: 323-720-8810
Fax: 323-722-7826
www.scofield.com

Provides engineered systems for coloring, texturing, and improving the performance of architectural concrete. Coloring admixtures, floor hardeners, colored cementitious toppings, stains and stain enhancer, curing agents, sealers, coatings, repair products, and texturing tools are among its products.

QC CONSTRUCTION PRODUCTS

232 South Schnoor Ave.
Madera, CA 93639
Phone: 800-453-8213
www.qcconprod.com

Has a wide range of colorants for achieving hues ranging from subtle to bright, such as integral coloring, patina stain, dry-shake color hardener, and a penetrating water-based tinting compound. Also sells protective sealers, floor cleaners, and stripping products for removing worn sealer and finishes.

RARE EARTH LABS

527 Russell Ave.
El Dorado, AR 71730
Phone: 800-664-0670
Fax: 870-862-9840
www.rareearthlabs.com

Sells concentrated concrete and masonry acid stains that can be diluted with water to achieve various color intensities, ranging from a watercolor-wash effect to rich earth tones.

SPECIALTY CONCRETE PRODUCTS INC.

1327-T Lake Dogwood Drive
West Columbia, SC 29170
Phone: 800-533-4702
Fax: 803-955-0011
www.scpusa.com

Manufacturer of acid stains, stamped concrete products, sealers, and resurfacing materials for new concrete construction or renovation. Also offers hands-on decorative concrete training classes monthly at its South Carolina facility.

SUPERSTONE INC.

1251 Burlington St.
Opa-Locka, FL 33054
Phone: 800-456-3561
Fax: 305-681-5106
www.superstone.com

Supplies a broad range of products for concrete resurfacing and beautification, including a penetrating chemical stain that simulates the look of weathered stone, marble, or tile. Other products include liquid colorant, integral color, solvent-based acrylic sealers, resurfacing and crack repair polymers, and texturing mats.

SURFACE GEL TEK

8201 East Highland Ave.
Scottsdale, AZ 85251
Phone: 480-970-4580
Fax: 480-421-6322
www.surfacegeltek.com

Sells a gelled acid product that works with vinyl stencil materials for precision decorative stenciling of concrete. It can also be used to open up steel-troweled concrete surfaces and to produce a uniform etched surface for improved penetration and adhesion of subsequent products.

VAPORPRECISION INC.

2941 West MacArthur Blvd., Suite 135
Santa Ana, CA 92704
Phone: 800-449-6194
Fax: 714-549-8245
www.vaportest.com

Supplies calcium chloride kits, tools, and technical support for moisture vapor testing of interior concrete slabs.